MANAGE YOUR CONTENT AND DEVICES

Learn The Secrets of Android and Unlock The Full Potential of Smartphones, Tablets and Smart Watches.

ORVILLE CAROL FRED

Get the audiobook version of this title for free with a 30 days Audible trial.

From US

From UK

Discover 7 Magnificent Things you can do with your Android Phone

Table of Contents

Thanks again for choosing this book, I'd really love to hear your thoughts.

Make sure to leave a short review on Amazon if you enjoy it.

INTRODUCTION

The holidays, oh the holidays. Whatever sort of winter celebration you favor (I prefer Festivus), late December is a great time to relax and plan for the new year.

That means now is a great time to think about that crazy tiny computer in your pocket and the measures you can take to make it even more powerful – because guess what? A few minutes of tweaking now will make your life immensely easier throughout 2021. Consider it a gift to yourself that goes on giving and, best of all, doesn't cost you a thing.

If you missed any of them the first time around or simply

didn't have the opportunity to try them all, here are some of my favorite productivity-boosting Android ideas from Android Intelligence articles and other related sources.

Pour yourself a cup of cocoa, dust out the Festivus pole, and give yourself the gift of beautifully calibrated technology.

Have you ever considered that there is more to your Android smartphone than what the manufacturer has told you it should be? You are not mistaken! We'll show you some Android tricks that will absolutely blow your head in this book!

It is no secret that we live in a technologically advanced world!

High-tech products are constantly being developed and updated – it's insane! Technology has made it possible to combine and use mechanical and hardware components. How? By implementing software systems. Which, in turn, gave us the gift of operating systems, allowing us to all use technology through interacting gadgets.

As you can see, Microsoft Windows was the dominant operating system for many decades! Even now, it remains a commonly used operating system, particularly in laptop computers. Microsoft Windows has been dethroned as the most popular operating system as smartphones have grown in popularity.

The Android OS

Android is the most popular mobile operating system in the world. With such a large market presence, it's no surprise that the Google Play Store has millions of apps for Android users. You can use some apps in conjunction with various tactics to fully utilize the capabilities of your Android phone. But it doesn't end there if you're wondering how.

CHAPTER 1: MULTITASK LIKE A PRO BY USING TWO APPS AT THE SAME TIME ON YOUR ANDROID PHONE

The split-screen mode on Android isn't always obvious, but using it can prevent you from switching between apps frequently.

Switching between a text discussion and Yelp as you decide what to order for delivery with your companion is a convenient yet time-consuming method to multitask, especially on an Android phone. It's functional, but there's a better approach. Android includes built-in functionality that allows you to run two apps on your screen at the same time, allowing you to take advantage of all the screen real estate than today's smartphones come with.

Using the same example as before, you display Yelp and Messages in split-screen mode, allowing you to browse menus on the top half of your screen while exchanging links in a text chat on the bottom half. It's really convenient and simple to use, requiring only a couple of taps to activate.

Keep in mind that depending on the phone you use, the split-screen mode may look or perform differently. Samsung, for example, had its own implementation long before Google officially included it in Android.

Here's Where To Find Split-Screen Mode On An Android Device:

1. You're a pro at getting to the proper location if you've ever forced an app to quit. Tap the app switcher icon to see all of your open apps if you haven't yet switched to Android 10's gestures. Swipe up from the bottom of your screen and pause approximately halfway up if you're using gestures.

2. After that, locate one of the apps you wish to use and hit the app icon at the top of its thumbnail, then Split Screen.

3. The app switcher view will remain displayed on the bottom half of your screen as that app slides to the top.

You can either go to your home screen or the app drawer to find the second app from there.

4. You are not obligated to use both apps on your screen at the same time. There's a handle in the middle of the line that separates them that you can pull up or down to resize the apps. If you're working on a spreadsheet and need information from an email, for example, you can reduce Gmail only to show what you need while still viewing more cells.

Split-screen mode isn't supported by all apps, and there's no way to know if one will function without trying it.

Samsung Phones Can Do Even More

On a Samsung device, there are a few different ways to multitask. You can get the same split-screen feature and functionality by following the methods indicated above. You do, however, have the option to open the file in a pop-up window.

The software is reduced to a small window that you can move around the screen and resize as needed in the pop-up view.

You can make your own split-screen with Samsung's Edge Panel, a slender side window that lets you access apps and more from any screen. Shortcuts for launching two apps simultaneously on demand. You can, for example, open the browser on top and your preferred chat app on the bottom. To personalize your options, click to Settings > Display > Edge screen > Edge panels on your phone.

How To Enable Split-Screen Multitasking On Android 10

The way we use and navigate our devices has changed with Android 10. Of course, the most significant difference from prior Android versions is the redesigned navigation system, which now entirely depends on gestures rather than buttons.

The navigation system, however, is not the only feature that Android 10 introduces. In Android, Google also altered the way we multitask. To use split-screen in earlier versions of the OS, you had to have several applications running in the background. Then you'd drag two applications to the top and bottom of your screen, and you'd be multitasking in no time.

Swiping, on the other hand, with Android 10 closes the program rather than moving it to split-screen mode. As a result, some users are perplexed by the new system. But don't panic; utilizing split-screen on Android 10 is just as easy as it's always been. It's simply done a little differently this time.

How To Multitask On Android 10

Here's how to utilize two applications on Android 10 at the same time:

- Start the app that you wish to use in split-screen mode.

- Navigate to the Recent Apps screen. This depends on the navigation method you're using (swipe up the home bar if you're using gestures, swipe up from the pill if you're using two-button navigation, or press the recent (square) button if you're using three-button navigation).

- Locate the program that you wish to use in split-screen mode.

- Depending on your device, tap the three-dot menu or the app icon.

- Select Split screen.

- Now, from the app switcher, select another app and tap it.

- Both applications will now be in split-screen mode, allowing you to multitask.

- I should also note that in split-screen mode, you may select the portion of the screen that each program will utilize. However, because this may not function correctly in landscape mode, you should only perform it in portrait mode.

How To Resize Apps In The Split-Screen Mode

Here's how to resize apps while in multitasking mode on Android 10:

- Check that both programs are still in multitasking mode.

- Tap and hold the black center bar, then drag it up or down to increase the percentage of the screen that one app occupies.

If you drag the bar to the top, the app on the bottom will launch in full screen, thus closing the split-screen mode. If you move the bar to the bottom, the opposite will happen.

How To Lock People Out Of Specific Apps On Android

If you wish to lend your phone to someone else, you should restrict them from launching your applications. WhatsApp, Gmail, and the image gallery might all include sensitive information that you wish to keep secret. But don't worry. You can secure critical information from prying eyes with an app lock function.

Several smartphone manufacturers include the app lock functionality as part of their customized Android skin. We've described how to utilize the app lock functionality on the most popular Android skins below. But what if your phone is running pure Android and you still don't have the app lock feature? We've addressed your issues as well, and we'll teach you how to work around this issue.

Use the Built-in App Lock feature

As previously said, if your smartphone is produced by one of the brands listed below, you may not even need to hunt for a third-party app. Using the app lock functionality built into the app is also intrinsically more secure than using a third-party solution.

On Samsung devices, how to utilize App Lock

- Samsung App Lock is a feature that allows you to lock your apps to prevent them from being

- Lower-end/mid-range It's possible that Samsung phones will include them.

- Pre-installed S Secure Software Lock app.

It may be accessed using the following menu:

- Navigate to Settings.

- Scroll down to Advanced Options.

- Look for the Lock and mask applications option.

- If you do not see this option, you must install the S Secure software from the Google Play Store.

- Check again once the app has been installed, and you should see the Lock and mask applications option - tap on it.
- Toggle the switch to the On position.
- You will now be able to select a pattern, PIN, password, or Face unlock.
- Choose your preferred choice and configure it.
- Once the lock type has been selected, choose Locked applications.
- The screen will be blank because you just put it up. In the top right corner, tap the Add button.
- You will now see a list of applications with a checkbox next to each one.
- Choose the applications you want to lock.
- Return to the Locked applications screen, and the selected apps will now be visible.
- Return to the applications carousel, and you'll notice a lock icon next to the app you choose.

Lock Apps using Samsung Secure Folder

The App Lock function may not be available to you depending on where you reside and which smartphone model you are using. Instead, your smartphone is likely to include a function called Samsung Secure Folder. You may use this functionality to save applications, photos, and other data in the Secure Folder. A different code protects this from your primary account. Even with a USB cord and a PC, you can't access the data in the protected folder.

To access Secure Folder:

- Open Settings
- Tap Biometrics and security.
- Tap Secure Folder.

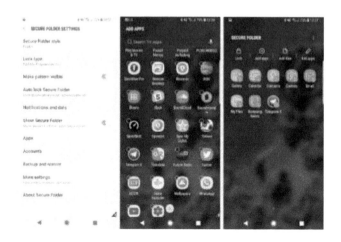

When you use the Secure Folder, you will need to re-install WhatsApp or other apps. Notifications are delivered to your main profile from the Secure Folder. A sophisticated settings menu makes it simple to configure your chosen privacy settings. In exchange, you get system-level security, making it impossible even for resourceful spies.

On OnePlus devices, how to utilize App Lock

If you possess a OnePlus smartphone, you already have an app lock function built-in.

Here's how to enable it.

- Open Settings.
- Tap on Utilities.
- Tap App locker.
- Choose a screen lock method.
- Choose how you want alerts to appear on the lock screen and then press Done.
- This will take you to the App Locker menu. Select Add applications from the menu.
- From the list, choose the apps you'll require.
- Return to the list and you'll see the selected apps.

How To Use App Lock-On Xiaomi / Poco Smartphones

If you have a Xiaomi/Poco/Redmi smartphone running MIUI, follow these steps to enable the app lock feature:

- Scroll down and tap on Apps under Settings.

- Select App lock.

- You will be given the opportunity to enable the function.

- To make your life easier, Xiaomi pre-selects applications that it believes you will want to lock.

- Turn on the switch.

- If your phone had a lock code, it would prompt you to input it right away.

- The following screen will provide a list of apps that may be secured; pick those that you want and then tap Use App lock.

- You may be prompted to input your Mi Account details on the next screen. However, it is not required.

- Select Not now.

- To gain access to protected applications, you must enter a PIN on the following page. You may choose between a PIN, a pattern, and a password.
- That's all!

On Huawei devices, how do you utilize App Lock?

This is what you need to do to use the App lock function on Huawei smartphones:

- Navigate to Security in Settings.
- Select App Lock.
- You will now be prompted to choose a password for App Lock. Select either your current Lock screen password or a new PIN.
- Enter your new PIN.
- On the next page, if you have enrolled in your fingerprint, you can choose to use it to unlock applications as well.
- You will now be presented with a list of applications that can be locked. Select the ones you want.

How to use App Lock on Oppo/ Realme smartphones

If you have an Oppo or Realme smartphone, the method for enabling the app lock function is the same:

- Select Privacy from the Settings menu.

- Select App lock from the Privacy option.

- You will now be prompted to create a Privacy password.

- Tap Next after entering a password of your choosing.

- You will now see a list of applications that have been pre-selected to be locked. Choose which applications you wish to be locked.

- On the next page, you can choose to employ biometric techniques if you have them enabled.

Use a launcher that supports App Lock

If your smartphone lacks an in-built App lock function, one solution is to switch to a launcher that supports the feature. This is also an option for smartphones that run the native Android operating system. If you don't want to give up the standard Android UI, you'll have to seek alternatives.

Apex Launcher is our pick for a launcher that features the App lock functionality.

Running stock Android? Download an App Lock app from the Google Play Store

If your phone runs stock Android, your best bet is to download and install specialized software for app locking. One of the best programs I found was from Norton, the creator of the famous antivirus product. The program is named Norton LifeLock, and it is available for download from the Google Play Store.

After you've installed the app, you'll need to go through the setup procedure.

You may be required to give numerous rights, such as display above other apps and accessibility.

Choose a locking technique (pattern on PIN).

You may choose which applications to lock.

Set up a user or guest account.

If you're not comfortable utilizing third-party software, your only other choice is to use Android's 'Guest mode' function.

To enable this, you will need to do this:

- Open Settings.
- Tap Multiple users.

- Toggle the switch to on.
- Tap on Add guest.

That's all there is to it. When you need to give over your phone to someone else, you may now switch to Guest mode, and they will not have access to your personal data or applications. They will either have their own Google account or none at all. They will only be able to install applications from the Play Store and will not be able to make phone calls, send SMS messages, or access other people's data. Of course, this includes your apps. You can even hand the phone to another person on a regular basis if you set it up as a user rather than a visitor, and they may keep their data on it as well.

CHAPTER 2: USING GOOGLE SMART LOCK ON YOUR ANDROID DEVICE

Google Smart Lock, often known as Android Smart Lock, is a useful collection of features included with Android 5.0 Lollipop. It eliminates the need to continuously unlock your phone after it has been idle by allowing you to create circumstances in which your phone may securely be unlocked for lengthy periods of time. The functionality is accessible on select Android smartphones and apps.

On-Body Detection

When you hold your smartphone in your hand or pocket, this function recognizes it and keeps it unlocked. When you set your phone down, it locks automatically, so you don't have to worry about prying eyes.

Trusted Places

It's extra aggravating when your smartphone keeps locking up on you when you're at home. Enabling Smart Lock fixes this by setting Trusted Places, such as your house, office, or any other location where you are comfortable keeping your device unlocked for an extended period of time. This function, however, necessitates the activation of GPS, which depletes your battery faster.

Trusted Face

Do you recall the Face Unlock feature? This feature, which debuted with Android 4.0 Ice Cream Sandwich, allows you to unlock your phone using face recognition. Unfortunately, the function was untrustworthy and easily fooled by using a photo of the owner. This function, now known as Trusted Face, has been enhanced and included in Smart Lock; with it, the phone utilizes facial recognition to allow the device's owner to engage with alerts and unlock the device.

Trusted Voice

You may utilize the Trusted Voice function if you use voice commands. Once you've enabled voice detection, your smartphone will be able to unlock itself when it detects a voice match. This function isn't completely secure: anybody with a similar voice to yours might unlock your smartphone. When using it, be cautious.

Trusted Devices

When you connect to a new Bluetooth device, such as a wristwatch, Bluetooth headset, vehicle radio, or another accessory, your device asks if you want to add it as a trusted device. If you opt-in, your phone will stay unlocked each time it connects to that device. When you connect your smartphone to a wearable device, such as the Moto 360 wristwatch, you can view messages and other alerts on the wearable and reply to them on your phone. Trusted Devices is a fantastic feature if you often use a Wear OS device (previously Android Wear device) or another accessory.

Chromebook Smart Lock

This feature may also be enabled on your Chromebook by heading to advanced settings. Then, if your unlocked Android phone is handy, you may unlock your Chromebook with a single tap.

Saving Passwords With Smart Lock

Smart Lock also has a password-saving function that works with compatible Android apps and the Chrome browser. Go to Google settings to activate this function; you can also switch on auto sign-in to make the procedure easier. Passwords are stored in your Google account and are available anytime you login in on a supported device. You can prevent Google from remembering passwords from specific applications, such as banking or other apps that hold sensitive data, for more protection. The main drawback is that not all apps are compatible, necessitating involvement from app creators.

HOW TO SET UP A SMART LOCK

Follow the instructions below to install Smart Lock on your Android device.

On-Body Detection in Android Smart Lock: How To Set It Up

On-body detection is a Smart Lock feature that keeps your phone unlocked when it is on you. This condition detects if your phone is moving or resting idly by using the built-in accelerometer and other sensors (motionless).

When you use your phone while it is in motion, the on-body detection condition is met, and your phone remains unlocked.

If you set your phone down and there is no activity, this condition is false, and your phone is locked:

- Navigate to the Android Settings app.
- Scroll down and select the Security & lock screen option.
- On the subsequent page, select Smart Lock. This is where you may customize the different Smart Lock techniques.
- Continue by confirming your device's PIN.

- On the following page, select the On-body detection technique.

- At the top, you'll find a toggle labeled Off. To enable the On-body detection technique, flip this switch to the ON position.

- To activate the technique, tap Continue on the popup.

- This method does not rely on the user's identification to be verified. As a result, regardless of who uses it, your phone will remain unlocked and usable. You should only use this procedure if you're certain you're the only one who has access to the phone.

You may disable this function by switching the toggle in the second to final step above to OFF.

How Do I Add Trusted Locations To My Android Smart Lock?

You may utilize the Trusted Places feature to keep your smartphone unlocked in specific areas. You may manually define your trusted locations using this functionality. Your phone remains unlocked while you are in those areas.

When the phone senses that you are not in a trusted place, it will lock.

This function uses Google Maps and your phone's GPS to assist in locating you.

You can designate several locations as trustworthy locations:

- Open the Settings app.
- Tap the Security & Lock screen, then Smart Lock.
- Select the option labeled Trusted locations.
- You may now include a trustworthy location in this approach. To do so, select the Add trustworthy location option.
- The Google Maps screen will appear. Move the marker to the location you wish to use as a trusted location. Then, at the bottom, press Select this place.

- Your phone will prompt you to name your location. Enter a name that will help you remember this location and press OK.

- To add another location, select the Add trustworthy place option once again.

- When you are in the designated places, Smart Lock will keep your smartphone unlocked.

- If your address has changed, you can update your trusted places. Tap a place and then choose Edit Address. Then, select a new place by tapping Select this location.

- If you no longer wish to maintain a location in trusted locations, tap it and choose Delete.

How To Use Android Smart Lock To Set Up Trusted Devices

When one of your trusted devices is linked to your phone, Smart Lock allows you to keep your phone unlocked. This approach may be used with any Bluetooth-enabled device.

This includes the Bluetooth system in your automobile, headphones or earbuds, Bluetooth-enabled smartwatches, and other Bluetooth-enabled devices. Keep in mind that because this technique relies on Bluetooth, your Bluetooth devices must be within 100 meters of your phone in order for it to remain unlocked.

On your phone, go to Settings > Security & lock screen > Smart Lock.

Select Trusted devices from the drop-down menu.

In the lower-right corner, click the Add Trusted Device button.

Your phone will display the Bluetooth devices you've previously used. To connect to one of these devices, tap it. If you wish to utilize a device that you haven't previously linked to your phone, you must first go into Settings and pair with that device.

Tap Yes, Add in the popup that appears on your screen.

When the Bluetooth gadget connects to your phone, it unlocks and stays unlocked.

You may add another trusted device by selecting Add trusted device and completing the same steps as before.

If you do not want to use your Bluetooth device to unlock your phone, choose Remove Trusted Device from the list.

Keep your trusted Bluetooth devices with you at all times, as anybody with access to any of them can use them to unlock your phone.

How To Set Up Facial Recognition In Android Smart Lock

The facial recognition tool scans your face and compares it to previously recorded face information. If the faces match, your phone will unlock.

Most phones will warn you that this technique is less secure than using a PIN or password. Someone with a similar face to yours can also unlock your phone. As a result, you should exercise caution when employing this approach.

On your smartphone, go to Settings > Security & lock screen > Smart Lock.

Choose the option Trusted face.

To begin configuring the technique, tap Set Up in the bottom-right corner.

Read the suggestions about how to use your phone's camera to scan your face. Then, at the bottom, hit Next.

You'll see the view from your camera. Make sure your face fits inside the circle by pointing your camera at it.

Wait for your phone to scan your face and upload it to the system.

When your face has been uploaded to Smart Lock, tap Done. Simply switch on your phone to access this function. When you look at your front camera, your phone will unlock.

If your phone won't unlock for any reason, go to Smart Lock and hit Improve face matching to snap another photo of yourself in better lighting.

You may turn off this function by selecting Remove trusted face. This will erase your facial information from your phone.

If your phone doesn't open with your face, you can use your PIN or pattern to access it.

Entering a PIN or swiping a pattern to unlock a phone is considered tedious and time-consuming by many users. Smart Lock takes care of that by keeping your phone unlocked in preset trustworthy conditions.

How To Recover Deleted Notifications On Android

Things were a little more difficult before Android 11 if you wanted to look at past notifications. Users with android Phones 11 may, on the other hand, easily retrieve and view recent notifications on their Android smartphone. It should be noted that this functionality is not currently accessible for many Android UIs that are already running Android 11. If you have a phone with an Android UI that doesn't support this functionality natively, there are a few applications that can help you out.

How to access Android notification history

How to View Your Android 11 Notification History (Stock Android). Turn on the 'Notification History feature' to guarantee that you have access to all alerts on your smartphone, even if you thought you removed them. When you're finished, the program will keep track of every notice you've gotten in the last 24 hours. Even if you mistakenly swipe away notifications from the drop-down tray, you may still view them if you have this feature enabled and check it within 24 hours.

First, let's look at how to enable the 'Notification History' function on stock Android smartphones running Android 11:

- On your Android smartphone running stock Android 11, navigate to the 'Settings menu.

- Scroll down the menu to 'Apps & Notifications,' then choose and press 'Notifications.'

- Tap 'Notification history,' and then toggle the 'Use notification history' toggle to the on position.

- Your phone will now retain a log of all alerts, which may be accessed for the next 24 hours.

If you have already enabled the 'Use notification history' option, you will be able to see a complete record of notifications received by your phone in the last 24 hours. Once activated, the list of alerts will be empty for a while. Once you've received many alerts, you may use this menu to touch a notice, which will send you directly to the app in question.

On Color OS 11, how do I see old notifications?

Users of Oppo smartphones running Color OS 11 may also view deleted notifications. The processes are identical to what we observed on vanilla Android. This also implies that the user must enable the 'Notification history' function in order to begin logging data. Follow these instructions to view Color OS 11's notification history.

Go to the Settings menu.

Tap 'Notification & Status Bar,' then 'Manage Notifications.' Choose 'More.'

Tap 'Notification History,' and make sure the notification history toggle is turned on.

Getting access to deleted notifications on Android 10 or older might be difficult.

How to View Your Android 10 Notification History

The notifications log feature was launched with Android 4.3 Jellybean and is still available from Android Lollipop to Android 10. You can examine deleted notifications in the Notification Log, but it is only available through an almost-secret widget. To unlock the widget and restore your lost alerts, it appears that you must first activate the Developer Options on many phones.

Navigate to Settings > About Phone and repeatedly tap the Build number to enable developer options. After 3 or 4 clicks, an on-screen notice will appear informing you that you are now a developer (it also adds a new section in your Settings menu).

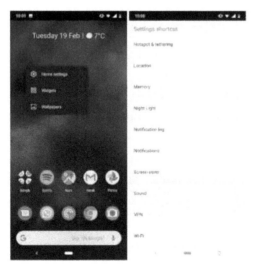

Steps

- Long-tap an empty area on your Android home screen, then choose Widgets.

- To access to the Settings shortcut widget, swipe left or scroll down the widget menu.

- Long-tap the widget until your home screens display, then drag it to a home screen of your choice.

- Scroll down and choose Notification log from the Settings shortcut menu that opens.

- A Notification log shortcut will appear on your home screen. Simply tapping this will give you access to your notification history and the ability to retrieve any missed alerts.

- When you're in the notification log, you'll see current notifications in white and notifications you've closed in grey. You may tap the grey alerts as you usually would, and you'll be transported directly to the source of the notice.

Recover Deleted Notifications Using Third-Party Apps

This feature isn't available on all Android phones that have their own user interface. It is at the discretion of the OEM, who may have opted not to add this functionality. There might be another method to view deleted notifications, and the easiest way to find out is to search for your phone's model and look up how to get deleted notifications. If it does not work, you may always use a third-party app to access the notification log.

In this section, we'll look at various third-party applications that might help you retrieve lost notifications from your Android device:

1. Notification History Log

This app, as the name implies, provides the basic but vital goal of keeping a record and preserving a log of your alerts. Android devices that lack a built-in notification log can benefit from this software in a simple and effective manner. It is compatible with any Android smartphone, regardless of custom UI.

Notification History Log is an efficient solution that does its job well. It keeps track of all alerts received in a single day. If you wish to keep a record for a longer period of time, you must purchase the app's paid premium edition. There is an Advanced History Settings section where you can view a list of applications that give you alerts on a daily basis. You can uninstall applications whose alerts aren't critical, and you don't want to maintain a record of them. In this way, you may personalize your notification log and keep track of only the most relevant alerts from the most crucial applications.

2. Notistory

Notistory is yet another free notification history software available on the Google Play Store. It includes a number of helpful features, such as the ability to access alerts that have been rejected or removed. In addition, the app has a floating notification bubble that can be used as a one-tap button to display all of your alerts. If you touch on these alerts, you will be taken to the app that created the notice.

The app works well with all apps. It also works with all Android smartphone brands and custom user interfaces. If you don't have a built-in function for the notification log, you can give it a shot.

3. Unnotification

This app is a little different from the others we've examined so far. Other applications allow you to retrieve lost or ignored notifications, but Unnotification protects you from dismissing or deleting essential alerts by accident. It is free to download from the Google Play Store. The software features a basic UI and is straightforward to install and use.

The following is a step-by-step instruction to utilizing Unnotification:

1. The first step is to download and install the app from the Google Play Store.
2. When you initially launch the app, it will request access to Notifications. Allow that since it can only restore deleted notifications if it has access to them in the first place.
3. Unnotification will be functioning immediately after you have granted it all of the necessary permissions.

4. Try dismissing any notifications you've received to see how the app works.

5. A new notice will appear in its place, asking you to confirm your decision to reject the message.

6. This gives you the opportunity to double-check your selection, preventing you from unintentionally removing an essential notice.

7. If you wish to remove a notice, ignore the second notification from Unnotification, and it will disappear after 5 seconds.

8. You can also add a tile to your Quick Settings menu that will restore the last removed notification by just pressing on it. Even after the above-mentioned 5 seconds have gone, it will restore the notice.

9. As previously said, there are some applications whose alerts are spam, and you should never restore them. You can block certain applications via a notice, but it will not function for them.

10. Simply launch the Unnotification app and press the Plus button to add an app to the Blacklist. You will now be shown a list of installed apps. You have the option of adding an app to the Blacklist.

11. In addition, you may navigate to the app's settings and modify various things to your liking. For example, you may choose how long you want the Unnotification to remain after dismissing any notification.

12. Any notice restored by Unnotification will function in the same way as the original notification. When you tap it, you'll be directed to the app that created it.

4. Nova Launcher

Although this is not a dedicated method for recovering lost alerts, it works very well. If your default UI does not include the notification log function, you can modify the UI. A third-party launcher offers a slew of personalized options to your phone.

Nova Launcher is a well-known and widely used third-party launcher. In addition to all of its helpful features and easy customization choices, it allows you to restore deleted alerts. Nova Launcher includes its own widget that allows you to view the Notification log, similar to the built-in widget on stock Android.

To add this widget, go to the "Activities" tab by tapping on a free spot on the home screen. Place this widget on the home screen by tapping and holding it. It will now provide a selection of alternatives for you to select from. Select Settings, and then select the "Notification Log" option. When you tap it, the widget will be placed on your home screen.

The notification log offered by Nova Launcher, on the other hand, has limited usefulness. It will just display the notification's subject or header and will not give any more information. The alerts will also not lead you to the original app that produced them in the first place. In certain situations, you may need to enable Developer settings in order for the Notification log to function on your device.

How to make an android smartphone backup

Android gives you the choice of either backing up everything to the cloud or doing a manual backup and saving it to your PC. When it comes to taking a backup to the cloud, you may do it in a variety of ways, including saving which applications are on your phone, as well as saving contacts and even messages to the cloud. However, not everything can be saved up to the cloud, so we'll show you how to backup your Android smartphone.

Create a Google Backup

First, we must ensure that we have enabled the option to backup our settings and other data to the cloud.

To do so, go to your device's Settings and select "Accounts & Sync."

Inside Accounts, you'll notice an option to "Auto-sync data," which must be activated. After that, go to Settings > Google and choose the Gmail ID you're using as your main on the phone.

From here, you'll find all of the choices for backing up to the cloud, including your contacts, photographs, app data, calendar events, Chrome tabs, Google Fit data, and more to your primary Gmail ID.

After that, go to Settings > Backup & Reset and tick the box next to "Back up my data."

Once you've done this, it will automatically preserve everything on your device, including WiFi passwords, Google Apps data, apps you've installed on your device, and other essential information that you can recover when you switch to a new device with the same Gmail ID.

Backup Media to your PC/Laptop

However, as previously stated, this technique of backup is insufficient because it does not save messages or media on your phone.

You will have to utilize the manual technique of backing up the data with a micro USB connection for this. However, if you have an SD card installed on your device, you may simply remove it and backup it on your PC. But, because it's difficult to locate a smartphone with a micro-SD card slot these days, let's stick to a more basic technique of utilizing a micro-USB cable. To transfer media files from your phone to your PC or laptop, connect the USB cable to your device and plug it into the PC.

Then, ensure that File Transfer is enabled on your device and use File Explorer on Windows or Finder on Mac to access your phone's internal storage.

Now, copy everything on your phone's internal storage and save it in a different folder on your PC where you can locate it later.

When you're finished copying everything, you may securely unplug the device from your PC, and the procedure will be finished.

Back up Text messages & Call Logs

If you have a lot of important text messages on your Android device, it is also vital that you backup your text messages. Third-party programs like SMS Backup+ can help you with this.

Install and launch the app on your smartphone, then hit the "Connect" option within the app. Then, choose your Gmail account, allow SMS permission to the app, and hit "Backup" to begin backing up your texts. This will save all of your text messages to Gmail, where they can be read in Gmail on any web browser under the "SMS" category.

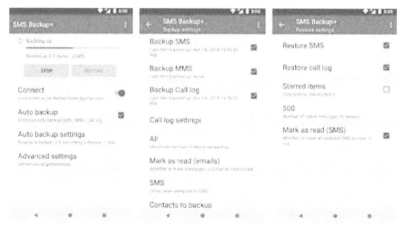

If you wish to restore the backed-up texts on your new smartphone, install the SMS Backup+ app and then press the "Restore" option. However, you will be prompted to set SMS Backup+ as your default SMS app, and you must respond by tapping "Yes." Not only will the software recover all of your messages, but it will also restore your call logs. The program's advantage is that after the messages are recovered, you will be requested to reinstall the SMS app that was previously set as the default.

Your android phone can be mirrored or cast to your tv.

It simply takes a few touches to mirror the display of your Android phone to a nearby television, whether you're watching a movie, making a video chat, or playing your favorite game.

Sharing photographs from a recent summer trip or joining a workout class at your local gym via Zoom may be a frustrating job on an Android phone's tiny screen. Instead of gathering your friends and family around your phone, you can instantly cast or mirror your screen to a nearby TV with a few touches. You'll need the right tools to get the job done and avoid any neck pain.

Casting your screen is useful not just for a comfortable watching experience but also for playing a few games of Among Us or showing everyone the current TikTok trend you can't get enough of. What's the best part? You could already have all you require. If not, it's not too difficult to get started. Here's how to start mirroring or casting the screen of your Android phone or tablet to your TV.

To mirror your Android phone to your TV, you'll need the following items.

To begin, you'll need an Android device running Android 5.0 or later. Because that version of Android was launched in 2014, the chances are that your phone or tablet is running a more recent version of Android. You can find out by opening the Settings app, heading to About phone, and searching for the Android version.

In addition to an Android phone or tablet, you'll need a Google Chromecast streaming device, such as the recently released Chromecast with Google TV, a TV with built-in Chromecast, or a smart display like the Google Nest Hub. If you're not sure whether your TV supports Chromecast, the simplest way to find out is to see if it appears as an available casting device when you use one of the methods below.

Using the Google Home app, cast your screen.

The Google Home app is the most dependable and consistent way to reflect your Android phone's screen. It's probably already installed if you've set up any of Google's smart speakers, Nest Wifi, or Chromecast devices. If not, you may get it from the Google Play store.

Select the Chromecast device you wish to utilize in the

Home app. At the bottom of the screen, there will be a Cast my Screen button; tap it. You must accept the popup informing you that whatever is on your phone's screen will be viewable to anybody in the room on your TV. If your device isn't designed for mirroring, you may get a second question. When I've encountered the warning, I've had no trouble casting my screen. To stop mirroring your screen, go to the Home app and press the Stop mirroring button.

There is a simpler method, however it is dependent on your phone.

Using the Home app isn't difficult, but there's an even simpler way: In the fast settings window, select the Casting shortcut. To access the quick settings panel, swipe down from the top of your Android phone or tablet's display. If you don't see a Screen Cast option, you may need to touch on the pencil symbol to change what is and isn't visible in your quick settings panel.

Once you've located the Screen Cast option, click it and then select the device from the list to which you wish to mirror your display. Your phone may take a few seconds to connect to the Chromecast-enabled device, but once it does, your screen will appear on your TV. Stop casting by repeating the procedures we just went through.

In the quick settings panel, not every phone has a cast button option. It's unclear why, so don't give up if your phone doesn't have the shortcut option. You may still use the Home app to mirror your phone.

Remember that when you mirror your screen, everything that appears on the display of your phone or tablet will also appear on the TV. That is, any alerts and notifications, as well as their contents, will be aired for everyone to see. To reduce interruptions to a minimum, I recommend turning on Do Not Disturb. Also, because there may be a latency between your phone and TV when streaming, stick to slower games and avoid more demanding titles like Fortnite.

CHAPTER 3: HOW TO CHANGE THE SIZE OF TEXT, ICONS, AND MORE IN ANDROID

Customization is one of the characteristics that differentiates Android, although it serves a purpose other than aesthetics. If you have difficulty seeing anything, you may change the size of icons, text, and other elements. We'll demonstrate how.

Depending on the version of Android you're running (and the type of phone), you may be able to modify only the text size or even make the entire screen bigger. We'll go through all of those choices in this article, as well as a few additional things you can do to make your phone easier to view.

How to Change the Icon & Font Size on Android

When you alter the size of the app icons on Android, you also modify the size of the text. This is because the "Display Size" options expand the whole phone interface.

First, depending on your phone, slide down once or twice to access the Quick Settings option. To access the system settings, click the gear symbol.

Go to the "Display" settings now.

Look for the words "Display Size" or "Screen Zoom."

To change the size, drag the dot on the scale at the bottom of the screen. You can see how things will look by swiping through the previews.

That is all there is to it. As you move the dot on the scale, the display size changes in real-time.

How to Change Only the Text Size on Android

What if you simply want to change the font size? We can do it as well.

First, depending on your phone, slide down once or twice to access the Quick Settings option. To access the system settings, click the gear symbol.

Go to the "Display" settings now.

Look for the words "Font Size" or "Font Size and Style."

To change the font size, drag the dot on the scale at the bottom of the screen. At the top of the screen, you may see a preview of the text.

That is all there is to it. This option will modify the text size for your entire phone.

How to Temporarily Magnify the Screen on Android

Perhaps you don't want to enlarge everything on your phone permanently. The Magnification feature on Android allows you to zoom in on objects whenever you want.

First, depending on your phone, slide down once or twice to access the Quick Settings option. To access the system settings, click the gear symbol.

Scroll down to the section under "Accessibility."

Choose "Magnification." On a Samsung smartphone, you must first go to "Visibility Enhancements."

To activate the "Magnification Shortcut," toggle the switch on.

Android 12 included a visible Magnification Shortcut that floats on the screen's edge. You may use this to toggle between magnification modes.

Previous Android versions used a two-finger gesture to bring up the magnification modes. Swipe up with two fingers from the bottom of the screen.

In both situations, you may zoom in using Magnification in a variety of ways:

- Start Magnification to zoom in.

- Tap the screen to activate it.

- To move across the screen, drag two fingers.

- Zoom may be adjusted by pinching using two fingers.

To turn off magnification, use the shortcut.

- Start Magnification to zoom in briefly.

- Hold your finger down anywhere on the screen.

- To travel across the screen, drag your finger.

- To cease magnification, lift your finger.

On my android, how do I change the navigation buttons or gestures?

Many Android phones now have stunning full-screen navigation gestures. Maybe you don't like them or wish to try something else. We'll teach you how to alter the navigation buttons on Android in no time.

Regrettably, not all Android phones store the navigation button settings in the same location. In this lesson, we'll teach you how to use it with Samsung Galaxy and Google Pixel devices.

On a Samsung Galaxy Phone, Change the Navigation Buttons

- To begin, slide down from the top of your Samsung Galaxy screen and tap the gear symbol.

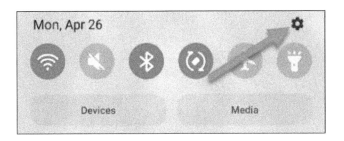

- Next, go to the Settings menu and choose "Display."

- Scroll down to the bottom of the options and tap "Navigation Bar."

Samsung Galaxy phones usually come with two options:

Buttons: Three buttons for "Recents," "Home," and "Back."

Swipe Gestures: Swipe up to return to Home, swipe up and hold to return to Recents, and swipe left or right to return to Back.

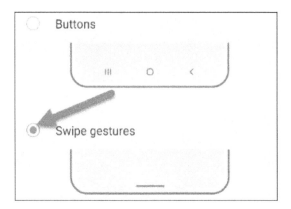

You may further tweak the motions by tapping "More Options."

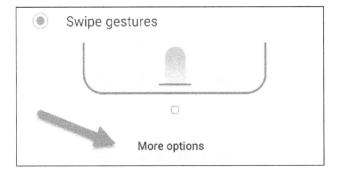

You may now add gesture bars to the three-button layout and change the gesture sensitivity.

When it comes to Samsung cellphones, that's all there is to it!

On a Google Pixel Phone, you may change the navigation buttons.

To access the Quick Settings toggles on a Google Pixel smartphone, slide down twice from the top of the screen and press the gear symbol.

Then, under the Settings menu, go to the "System" section. Select "Gestures" now.

The one we're looking for is "System Navigation."

There are two navigation choices available to you:

Gesture Navigation: Swipe up to return to the home screen, swipe up and hold to access Recents, then swipe left or right to return.

3-Button Navigation: Three buttons for "Recents," "Home," and "Back."

Lastly, if you use Gesture Navigation, you can tap the gear icon to adjust the sensitivity of the Back gesture.

Uninstall Multiple Apps At Once On Android

The Play Store has a plethora of applications, most of which are free to download. It's no secret that we frequently download apps on our Android devices without thinking about their purpose. Then, over time, such programs tend to take up a significant amount of space on our devices. This can also cause slowness; therefore, it's better to get rid of any unneeded programs. You can, however, simply uninstall undesirable programs from your Android device. However, if you have gathered a large number of applications that you desire to uninstall over time, it may be a time-consuming task.

Have you reached the end of your phone's storage capacity? This is most likely due to the fact that you have a lot of apps on your phone. The world is transitioning to an app-based model, similar to that of the Internet website. For example, if you want to pay your energy bill, your supplier may urge that you install their app, even if they have their own website, and it may also be paid through other service providers. Banks have also integrated utility bill payments into their net banking platforms and applications. The issue is that these applications take up space on your phone, and not everyone has a high-end phone. The majority of smartphones (70%) have 32 GB or 64 GB of storage. Installing such applications will take up space, and sometimes we don't even realize we've used up 90 percent of our capacity. If you are recording a video in this situation, you will be unable to do so due to storage constraints. You will have to install programs or remove data in such instances. Removing applications one by one takes time, and you may save time by bulk uninstalling apps on Android.

Uninstall Multiple Apps Android

Follow the steps outlined below to remove numerous apps on your Android device quickly:

- Open your mobile phone's app drawer.

- Tap to launch Google Play Store from the app drawer.

- Now, on the Google Play Store, select "My Apps & Games."

- You will now see a list of all the apps that are installed on your phone. The phone will also include sub-sections for Updates, Installed, Library, and Beta.

- Navigate to the Installed section and choose Storage. Then you'll see a list of applications that are currently installed on your phone.

- Now, choose the apps you don't want and press the "Free Up" button.

- Accept the request, and the undesirable applications will be removed from your Android phone immediately.

That is the typical method for removing numerous apps from an Android phone.

On the Play Store, there is a plethora of bulk uninstall

Android applications. But my favorites are ES File Explorer and Astro File Manager. These two programs are essentially file managers, although they can also perform a variety of other things.

Bulk Uninstall apps Using ES File Explorer:

- Install ES File Explorer from the Google Play Store.
- Launch ES File Explorer.
- To open the sliding menu, tap the Hamburger symbol.
- Navigate to Library >> App.
- Choose all of the programs you wish to remove. To choose several applications, long-press any one of them first. Then, touch all of the other applications you wish to choose.
- Uninstall should be clicked. All of the programs you've chosen will be removed one by one.

Bulk Uninstall apps Using Astro File Manager

- Install Astro File Manager from the Google Play Store.
- Once installed, launch Astro File Manager.
- To open the sliding menu, tap the Hamburger symbol.
- Navigate to Tools >> App Manager.
- Tap to open the Apps menu (Do not long-press, only tap)
- Select 'Uninstall.'

Lock phone borrowers inside one app

Limiting your device to a single app is an excellent way to allow your children to spend meaningful time on an Android phone or tablet. This ensures that your children spend important time on an age-appropriate or educational App while being secure from inappropriate material.

Lock Android Tablet to One App

The Pin Windows feature in Android, first introduced in Android 5.0, allows you to lock your Android phone or tablet to a single app.

This enables you to hand over your Android Phone or Tablet to your children without fear of Apps being removed or children being exposed to inappropriate information.

To lock your Android tablet to a single app, first enable the Pin Windows option on your Android device. Following that, you will be able to Lock Android Tablet to One App.

So, here are the techniques for locking an Android tablet to a single app:

1. **Turn on the Windows Pin feature on your phone or tablet.**

To enable the Pin Windows to function on your Android phone or tablet, follow the steps below:

- Navigate to Settings > scroll down and choose Lock Screen and Security or Biometrics & Security.
- Scroll down to the Other Security Settings option on the following screen.
- Tap the Pin Windows option on the Other Security Settings page.
- Enable the option to Pin Windows by sliding the slider to the ON position on the Pin Windows screen.

2. Setup Passcode for Screen Pinning Mode

The next step is to set up a Passcode for the Screen Pinning mode on your Android Phone or Tablet:

- Navigate to Settings > Security > Other Security Options > Windows Pinning.
- On the next screen, before unpinning, drag the slider next to Ask for a PIN to the ON position.

3. You can lock your Android tablet or phone to one app.

After you've activated the Pin Windows feature on your Android device, you may use the methods below to lock your Android phone or tablet to a single app:

- Open the app you wish to use to lock your Android phone or tablet.
- For example, launch WhatsApp to lock your Android phone or tablet to this one app and prevent it from being used by any other apps.
- Then, in the bottom-left corner of your smartphone, touch on the Recent Apps button.

- Tap on the App icon in the App pop-up and then on the Pin this App option.

Following this, only WhatsApp will be able to run on your Android device, and all other apps will be disabled.

4. On an Android tablet or phone, unpin an app.

After your kids have finished using your Android Tablet, you can unpin the App and take your device back to its normal mode:

- Hold down the Recent Apps and Back buttons at the same time.
- Enter your Lock Screen Passcode if requested to exit the Pinned Window and resume unfettered or regular use of your Android Phone or Tablet.

How to Use One-Handed Mode on Android

There's no disputing that phones have grown in size, sometimes absurdly so. Using a contemporary Android phone with one hand may be virtually difficult. That is where "One-Handed Mode" comes in, which is available on many Android phones.

If you're not familiar with "One-Handed Mode," it's a feature that moves the UI to the bottom of the screen to make it simpler to reach. This isn't a permanent solution, but it comes in helpful in some instances.

One-Handed Mode for Samsung Galaxy Phones

Samsung was among the first Android phone manufacturers to include One-Handed Mode. To get started, swipe down once from the top of the screen and tap the gear icon.

Go to the bottom of the Settings page and select "Advanced Features."

Choose "One-Handed Mode."

Toggle the top-of-the-screen switch to the on position.

Following that, you may configure how One-Handed Mode

is triggered. When utilizing gesture navigation, you can only select "Gesture." However, if you choose the three-button layout, you may also double-tap the home button.

In One-Handed Mode, you may move the smaller screen to the left or right by tapping the arrow symbol. You may also resize the screen by grabbing the corner. To leave, tap any empty screen space.

One-Handed Mode for Google Pixel Phones

In Android 12, Google Pixel phones received One-Handed Mode. To begin, swipe down from the top of the screen twice to display the Quick Settings menu, then press the gear symbol.

Scroll down and choose "System."

Select "Gestures" now.

Finally, select "One-Handed Mode."

Toggle the top switch to enable One-Handed Mode.

You also have a few more alternatives. Enable "Exit When Switching Apps" to have One-Handed Mode exit automatically when you leave an app.

Finally, you may provide a "Timeout" value to have One-Handed Mode leave after a specified amount of inactivity.

After that, you may access One-Handed Mode by swiping down on the home button or gesture bar. Swipe up on the same location or tap the blank space at the top of the screen to exit One-Handed Mode.

Even if you don't own a Samsung Galaxy or Google Pixel phone, there's a good possibility you have One-Handed Mode. You might be surprised if you look for it in the Settings! This is a useful skill to have.

How To Disable In-App Purchases On Your Android Device

While Android's in-app purchases feature makes it simple to purchase apps, you may wish to deactivate in-app purchases on your Android smartphone to avoid inadvertent and unwanted purchases. This section will walk you through the process of disabling or limiting in-app purchases on your Android device.

Disable In-App purchases On Android

The Android In-app Purchases feature is intended to simplify the process of purchasing apps and games on your Android smartphone. This feature allows you to buy anything on Google Play without having to enter your user name and password every time you make a purchase.

Leaving this option enabled on your smartphone, on the other hand, exposes you to the possibility of your children building up a huge bill on your Android phone by purchasing random applications and games.

As a result, this section will assist you with disabling in-app purchases on your Android device:

1. Go to the Google Play Store

Open the Google Play Store by tapping the shortcut on your phone's home screen or searching for it in the all applications list.

2. Tap on 3 Line Menu icon

Now, in the upper left corner of your screen, touch on the three-line menu symbol (See image below).

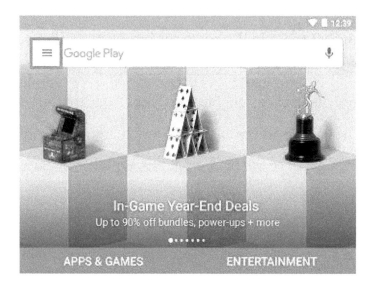

3. Tap on Settings

When you tap on the three-line menu symbol, a drop-down menu will appear; select Settings from the list.

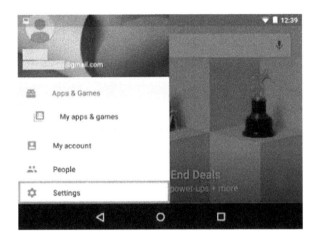

4. Change Require Authentication Frequency

Examine the options until you locate the User control sub-menu. Look for "Require Authentication for Purchases" in this sub-menu.

Now, tap on Require Authentication for Purchases, and you'll be given three options to choose from - we've provided a brief description of each option below.

Never: Purchases do not necessitate authentication.

Every thirty minutes: When you authenticate for a purchase, you may buy any type of digital material from Google Play for the following 30 minutes without having to authenticate again.

For all Google Play purchases made on this device: Every digital content purchase made through Google Play necessitates authentication.

On most Android devices, this setting is set to Every 30 minutes by default. This means that there is a 30-minute gap in which any of your children might inadvertently begin playing a paid game or downloading a paid app.

5. Change Authentication Setting

We recommend that you update the option to 'For all Google Play purchases on this device.'

6. Confirm Changes

To confirm the changes to the following settings, enter your Google account password.

After you make this change, anybody using your Android smartphone will be forced to provide their User Name and Password in order to make a Google Play purchase. This provides an extra layer of protection to your Android smartphone, avoiding inadvertent and accidental purchases.

Unlock Hidden Smartphone Features
with these Secret Codes

USSD, often known as "fast codes" or "feature codes," is an extra-UI protocol that enables users to access hidden functionality. This protocol was designed for GSM phones, but it's also found on CDMA phones (if that's a lot of acronym jargon to you, here's a refresher).

The USSD protocol enables you to use your smartphone's dialer to access secret capabilities you weren't aware of. However, there is some ambiguity that you should be aware of.

Coders have a long history of baking in hidden passages accessible only by entering a unique "key." As a result, the custom lives on in the mobile era.

These publicly accessible backchannels enable customers to interact directly with their service provider's computers and/or access their device's back-end functions. They're accessible by typing them into the phone's dialer (the screen you use to make a phone call), and they typically start and finish with the * or # keys, with a series of digits in between (there's a slim possibility they'd be reached by mistake).

Most individuals don't care about the performance of their local cell towers or their IMEI number (more on that later). Still, it's entertaining to mess with your phone and discover what hidden features it has.

If you're serious about trying them out, Google your phone's model and carrier + "USSD" for a customized, thorough list.

Field Mode: *3001#12345#*

To enter "Field Mode," type *3001#12345#* into your phone's dialer and then click the green call button. This will provide you information about local networks and cell towers.

You'll probably never need to know about the "Measured RSSi" of your local cell tower, but it's interesting to browse around for a while.

#0# *#0*# *#0*# *#0*# *#0*#

It's compatible with Android. This brings up a menu of several phone functions that may be accessed with a single button press (e.g., Sleep, Front Cam, Vibration).

Display your IMEI number: *#06#

To use it, enter the aforementioned code, then press the green call button to enter your IMEI number.

Your device's IMEI is unique. The number may be used to "blacklist" stolen devices or provide customer assistance, among other things.

*#67# *#67#

When you're busy or reject a call, you may use this code to see which number your phone is presently forwarding calls to.

This is most likely your carrier's voicemail service by default, but you may alter it to forward to a different phone number (a home number, office number, or third-party answering service, (for example). You may update this number on an iPhone by heading to Settings > Phone > Call Forwarding. Tap the Phone app > hamburger symbol > Settings > Call > More Settings > Call forwarding on Android (varies by OS).

Find Out More About Call Forwarding: This code triggered a pop-up on a Galaxy phone that explained how long before a call is routed to the message center. This code just displays the same information as *#67# on the iPhone, regardless of carrier.

Examine the Minutes You Have Available: *646#

This one seems to only work with postpaid plans. It is compatible with the Galaxy phone. Instead of displaying the information on a new screen, it sends a text message to the phone.

Check Your Bill Amount: On Android, dial *225# to get a text message with the current balance owing.

Hide Your Phone From Caller ID: #31#

It's compatible with Android. However, inputting this code resulted in a message saying that the Caller ID was deactivated. Enter *31# to reactivate your Caller ID.

*3282# It sends an SMS with billing information.

SMS Message Center: *5005*7672# This code will provide you with the number for your SMS message center.

Activate Call Waiting: *43# This code activates call waiting; to disable it, type #43#.

*#7353#

Only Samsung Galaxy models are compatible with this code. This mode works similarly to the General Test mode in that it displays a menu with a number of one-tap test prompts.

Firmware (Samsung Galaxy Only) *#1234# *#1234# *#1234# *#1234# *#1234# *#1234# *#1234# *#1234 However, it will inform you of the current firmware version of your phone. So, have some fun with it.

Most mobile phones are compatible with these codes. Most mobile phones should be able to use these codes. Depending on the supplier, some may not be functional.

Code	Function
press 1 for longer than one second	Call the mailbox number (mailbox number must be specified in the settings)
press # for longer than one second	Deactivate / Activate silent profile
#0#	On contemporary devices, you can access the service menu.
*#06#	Display the IMEI (International Mobile Equipment Identity)
#31#[number][dial]	Dial with own number being

	not displayed (replace [number] with the number to dial)
*31#[number][dial]	Dial with own number being displayed (replace [number] with the number to dial)
#33[dial]	Show status call locks
*43#[dial]	Turn on tall waiting
#43#[dial]	Turn off call waiting
*#43#[dial]	Show status of call waiting
*135#[dia]	Request own number (often does not work)
**04*[old Pin]*[new Pin]*[new Pin]#	Change Pin (do not enter [and])
**05*[PUK]*[neue Pin]*[neue Pin]#	Unlock Pin (do not enter [and])
**042*[old Pin2]*[new Pin2]*[new Pin2]#	Change Pin2 (do not enter [and])

**052*[PUK]*[new Pin2]*[new Pin2]#	Unlock Pin2 (do not enter [and])
*#0000#	Version of Software to Display (Nokia and Samsung devices)

Codes for charges:

Codes Function

*100#[Dial] Request number and balance (Prepaid)

*101#[Dial] Request number and balance (Prepaid)

SMS:

Send SMS delayed:

Enter the text at the beginning of the SMS.

*Later [seconds]#

Then substitute a number for [seconds], such as 10 for 10 seconds.

Example 1:

*Later 30#Hello, see you soon

Remember to leave a space between the second and the latter!

This isn't the case for all service providers.

Android's Hidden Codes

To enter these codes, open the default dialer app and use your chubby fingers to press the appropriate buttons.

Code	Description
##4636#*#*	The phone, the battery, and use statistics are all shown.
##7780#*#*	Only deletes application data and apps when you reset your phone to factory settings.
*2767*3855#	It is a full wipe of your phone, as well as a reinstallation of the phone's firmware.
##34971539#*#*	Displays all of the camera's details.
##7594#*#*	Changing the behavior of the power button—

	once the code is activated, it allows for straight power off.
##273283*255*663282*#*#*	To create a fast backup of all of your media files,
##197328640#*#*	Test mode for service activity is enabled.
##232339#*#* OR *#*#526#*#*	Tests on Wireless LAN
##232338#*#*	The Wi-Fi Mac address is shown.
##1472365#*#*	For a quick GPS test
##1575#*#*	Another kind of GPS test
##0283#*#*	Packet Loopback test
##0*#*#*	Test of the LCD display

##0673#*#* OR *#*#0289#*#*	Audio test
##0842#*#*	Backlight and vibration tests
##2663#*#*	Shows a touch-screen version.
##2664#*#*	The Touch-Screen test
*#9090#	Diagnostic configuration
*#872564#	USB logging control
*#301279#	Control Menu for HSDPA/HSUPA
*2767*3855#	Restore the device to its original state.
*#9900#	System dump mode
##7780#*#*	Restore the factory condition of the /data partition.

*#7465625#	Access phone lock status
*#12580*369#	Details on the software and hardware
##0588#*#*	Proximity sensor test
##3264#*#*	Ram version
##232331#*#*	Bluetooth test
##7262626#*#*	Field test
##232337#*#	The address of a Bluetooth device is displayed.
##8255#*#*	To keep track of the Google Talk service
##4986*2650468#*#*	Date firmware information for PDA, Phone, Hardware, and RF Call
##1234#*#*	Firmware information

	for PDAs and phones
##1111#*#*	FTA Software version
##2222#*#*	FTA Hardware version
##44336#*#*	Build time and change list number are displayed.
*#06#	Displays IMEI number
##8351#*#*	Voice dialing logging mode is enabled.
##8350#*#*	Voice dialing logging mode is disabled.
##778 (+call)	It opens the Epst menu.

CHAPTER 4: DISABLE EMERGENCY OR AMBER ALERTS ON ANDROID PHONE

Amber alert, also known as an emergency alert, is a helpful tool that alerts you to any potential hazard in your neighborhood, town, or city. It is a necessary function implemented by Android to bring things up to FCC standards. Your network service provider provides this emergency alert service. In the event of an emergency or a possible threat to your safety, you will hear a loud notification sound and receive a warning message.

What are the advantages of Amber or Emergency Alerts?

Various government departments, such as the Police Department, Fire Department, and Weather Department, can utilize the emergency alert system to inform you of a potential hazard in your neighborhood or town. Government agencies can send out a warning message with the assistance of a local network service provider. You receive an Emergency alert in the case of a hurricane, tsunami, earthquake, torrential rainfall, or other natural disasters so that you may take the required measures.

Another fantastic application for Amber alerts is to warn the community when someone goes missing. For example, if a child goes missing, the police department may now issue an emergency alert to everyone in the neighborhood and ask for aid. It significantly improves the chances of locating the missing person.

Why do you need to Disable the Emergency of Amber Alerts?

Although emergency notifications can be quite essential at times, they are hardly the most pleasant thing to hear at 3 a.m.

Emergency or Amber notifications will make a loud noise even if your phone is set to silent. Assume you're sound asleep or in the middle of a crucial meeting when your phone starts to ring loudly. It will astound you and cause a plethora of issues. There are times when you don't want to be disturbed, but one of them is when you receive emergency messages. Turning off the Emergency or Amber warning sound is the only way out.

Depending on the OEM, blocking Emergency or Amber notifications on an Android smartphone is done in a somewhat different way. We'll guide you through deactivating Amber Alert sounds on several Android smartphone brands in the next section.

HOW TO DISABLE EMERGENCY OR AMBER ALERTS ON STOCK ANDROID

Amber Alerts may be disabled from the device settings on Android handsets that run stock Android, such as the Google Pixel or Nexus. To see how, follow the steps outlined below:

- To begin, go to your device's Settings.
- Tap the Apps and Notifications option now.
- Scroll down to the bottom of the screen and select Advanced.
- Then, choose the Emergency notifications option.
- You will find a list of several types of emergency notifications here. Locate Amber Alerts and deactivate the toggle switch next to it. You may also turn off Alerts for Extreme and Severe risks if you wish.
- That's it; you're done. You will no longer get annoying Emergency notifications in the future.

On samsung smartphones, turn off emergency or amber alerts.

The procedure for disabling Emergency or Amber Alert sounds on Samsung devices differs somewhat from that of standard Android. Its emergency notification settings are accessible through its messaging app. However, before proceeding with the next steps, make sure that Samsung messages are selected as the default messaging app. After you've deactivated Amber alerts, you may use any other messaging app, and your decision will still be valid. After you've switched to Samsung Messages as your main messaging app, follow the steps below to turn off Amber Alerts:

The first thing you should do is open your iPhone's Settings app.

Then, select the Apps option.

Find the Samsung Messages app in the list of all installed applications on your smartphone and touch the Settings icon next to it.

Now choose Notifications from the drop-down menu.

In this window, disable the toggle switch next to the

Emergency notifications option.

You will no longer be awakened in the middle of the night by Amber alerts.

You may also access these options from inside the Messages app. Simply launch the Messages app (Samsung Messages) on your device and press the menu option (three vertical dots) on the upper right-hand side of the screen. Now, from the drop-down menu, select Settings and follow the procedures outlined above.

One advantage of utilizing a Samsung smartphone is the ability to temporarily mute Alert noises. Instead of fully deactivating Emergency alerts, you may merely silence the notification sound. As a result, you will be able to receive crucial safety warnings while being unaffected by them at random. These notifications will be delivered to your smartphone, and you may review them whenever you like. To temporarily stop Amber alert noises and silence notification sounds, follow the instructions below:

To begin, go to your device's Settings.

Then, select the Apps option.

Find the Samsung Messages app in the list of all installed applications on your smartphone and touch the Settings icon next to it.

Now, choose Emergency alert settings from the drop-down menu.

Simply turn off the switch next to the Alert sound choice.

As previously stated, Amber alert sounds can be configured to vibrate merely. This would still allow you to check the message without creating too much disruption.

Make sure that Alert reminders are turned on so that you receive timely reminders of the Emergency Alert messages you have received.

There is also the option to disable emergency notifications. However, we urge that you do not do so since you may lose out on important information.

Disable Emergency or Amber Alerts on LG Smartphones

LG is yet another popular smartphone brand. It also lets you simply turn off the Emergency or Amber alert sounds on your smartphone. This option is found in the Network and Internet settings. The following is a step-by-step instruction for disabling Emergency Alerts on your LG smartphone:

The first step is to go to Settings and choose the Network and Internet option.

Go to the Wireless Emergency Alerts section here.

Now, on the upper right-hand side of the screen, press the menu option (three vertical dots).

Select the Settings option from the drop-down menu.

Simply deactivate the toggle button next to the Amber Alerts option here.

Alternatively, you may turn off Amber Alerts in the Messages app. To see how, follow the steps outlined below:

To begin, use the Messages app on your device.

Now, on the upper right-hand side of the screen, press the menu option (three vertical dots).

Then, from the drop-down menu, pick the Settings option.

Tap the Emergency notifications option here.

Simply deactivate the toggle switch next to the Amber Alerts setting.

Disable Emergency or Amber Alerts on One Plus Smartphones

Amber alerts may be easily deactivated on a One Plus smartphone using the Messages app. It is a straightforward and painless procedure. To see how, follow the steps outlined below:

The first thing you should do is launch the Messages app on your iPhone.

Then, on the upper right-hand side of the screen, press the menu option (three vertical dots).

Now, from the drop-down menu, choose Settings.

Wireless notifications are an option you'll discover here. Tap it to activate it.

Look for Amber alerts and deactivate the toggle switch next to them.

That's it; you're done. You will no longer be bothered by abrupt and obnoxious alarm noises after the Amber alerts have been turned off.

CHAPTER 5: HOW TO TURN CAMERA FLASH ON OR OFF ON ANDROID

Almost every Android smartphone includes a flash to help the camera take better images. The Flash's aim is to give more light to ensure that the image is bright and visible. It comes in handy when natural lighting is inadequate if you are taking an outside photograph at night.

The use of flash is an essential aspect of photography. This is due to the importance of lighting in photography. It is, in fact, what distinguishes a good image from a terrible one. However, the Flash does not have to be used or turned on at all times. It sometimes puts too much light in the foreground, ruining the picture's attractiveness. It either washes out or gives a redeye appearance on the subject's features. As a result, it should be left to the user to determine whether or not to utilize Flash.

Depending on the scenario, conditions, and type of the photograph, one should be able to control whether or not the Flash is necessary. Fortunately, Android allows you to toggle the camera's flash on and off as needed. In this part, we will walk you through the process step by step.

How to Turn Camera Flash ON or OFF on Android

As previously said, turning on or off the camera flash on your Android is straightforward and can be accomplished with a few simple clicks.

To see how, follow the steps outlined below:

- To begin, use the Camera app on your device.

- Now, on the top panel of your screen, press the Lighting bolt icon.

- This will bring up a drop-down box where you may pick the status of your camera's flash.

- You have the option of leaving it on, off, automatic, or always on.

- Depending on the lighting conditions for the shot, choose whichever option you desire.

- By repeating the procedures outlined above, you may quickly move between different states and settings as needed.

How To Share Your Device Without Compromising Your Privacy With Android Guest Mode

If you often use your Android smartphone with other members of your household, you may not want them to be able to access your text messages or private photographs while you use it. You can always lock down the programs that contain your personal information, but this approach is not always failsafe. The good news is that there is a better way to prevent the borrower from having complete access to your personal information.

Guest Mode, which was first introduced in Android 5.0, allows users to share their smartphones without sacrificing their privacy. When you enable Android's Guest Mode, all of your data is safely stored in your user account and rendered inaccessible to the other party.

It's the same as performing a factory reset on your smartphone — you get a blank screen. But don't panic; you can quickly switch back to your user account (admin) and restore your data and settings.

How to Turn on Guest Mode on Your Phone

If you have never used Guest Mode on your device before, you will need to enable it. You may accomplish this by going into the settings on your phone.

- Open the Settings app on your phone.
- Scroll all the way to the bottom until you find System and tap on it.
- Choose "Multiple Users." Depending on your phone type, you may need to first touch on Advanced to view the option.
- Toggle the "Multiple Users" option on.
- That is all there is to it.

How to Turn on Android's Guest Mode

After you've activated Guest Mode on your phone, you may switch to it with a few clicks.

- Slide down on your display with two fingers to bring up the Quick Settings panel, then swipe down again to expand it.
- In the upper-right corner, tap the blue User symbol.

- Then, select Guest. The phone will transition to Guest Mode automatically.

- You may now pass the gadget along to anyone who needs to utilize it.

Except for the ones that were pre-loaded with the device, none of your installed applications will be accessible to your Guest. There will be no chance of the person currently using the phone snooping into your pictures, texts, or browser history because all settings will be restored to defaults as if the device had just been acquired.

To return to your user account, enter the Quick Settings panel and choose the admin user account, or simply select the "Remove Guest" option. This will erase all guest session data and return you to your own user account, albeit you must first unlock the device.

When a user quits Guest mode and then returns, they will be asked if they want to continue the current session or start a new one. The latter option allows Guests to resume where they left off, which is convenient for returning users. If a Guest wants to save their settings and other modifications for future use, the admin can establish a separate profile for them by clicking "Add User."

Configuring Guest Mode

When it comes to how the Guest mode works on your phone, you just have one option. Go to "Settings -> System -> Multiple Users -> Guest" once again. From there, you can activate the "Turn on phone calls" option to allow calls to go through even if another device is in use.

You may delete the Guest from your phone or switch to Guest mode from this option if you wish.

Using Android's Live Caption

Android 10 featured the Live Caption function, which automatically captioned any audio that was playing, first for selected Pixel phones. Later, the majority of Android OEMs included it in Android 10 phones (e.g., Samsung Galaxy S20 and Galaxy Note 20). Google enhanced this functionality much more in Android 11.

What is a Live Caption?

Live Captioning is a new function available on phones running Android 10 and above.

When the function is activated, the phone automatically recognizes audio and captions in real-time. You can utilize Live Caption even if your phone's audio is muted.

Live Caption creates captions in real-time based on the audio that is being played. Most Android applications support the functionality. However, some media and telephony apps may be excluded.

One of Android 10's big announcements was Live Caption, and the highly useful feature is now available on a broad range of Android devices as part of Android 11. Captions may be instantly added to any video, podcast, or audio message on your phone with Live Caption. It even works with self-recorded movies and audio files. There is no requirement for an internet connection for this to operate, and no data is sent to Google; everything is handled locally on the phone.

Does it sound right? Yes, it is! While not everyone will be able to use it, Live Captioning is now available on a larger variety of devices than ever before, including Google Pixels and Samsung smartphones running Android 11.

When to use Live Caption?

In Android 10 and Android 11, Live Caption may be used to caption audio from the following sources:

- Recordings
- Audio messages
- Videos
- Phone calls
- Podcasts

On Android 10 and Android 11, you may use this functionality to caption most audios.

How to turn on Live Caption

Because your phone won't arrive with Live Caption enabled by default, you'll have to jump through a few hoops to get it set up — but it's a very easy process, so don't be afraid.

On a Google Pixel or Samsung Galaxy phone, here's how to enable Live Captioning.

On a Google Pixel, enabling Live Caption.

For this tutorial, we utilized a Google Pixel 3a XL with Android 11.

Step 1: Go to Accessibility > Live Caption in Settings > Accessibility.

Step 2: Turn on Live Caption by toggling the option.

There are some extra settings here that may be of interest to many people. Language lets you change the language from English (where available), Hide Profanity conceals curses, Show Sound Labels displays labels for laughing, applause, and music, and Caption Calls lets you choose whether to caption calls Always, Never, or Ask Every Time.

Legal concerns have caused the Caption Calls functionality

to be delayed, as capturing a screenshot during a conversation with Live Captions enabled is nearly the same as recording a phone call. It is against the law to record a phone call without first informing all parties concerned. Of course, if someone does not want to be recorded, they are not required to accept the call. To work around this, Google Assistant informs everyone on the call at the start that the chat will be transcribed in real-time by Live Captions. As a result, you, Google, and the other party are all safe.

The most significant option here is arguably Live Caption in Volume Control, which adds a toggle button to your volume controls, enabling you to switch it on and off fast and simply.

After you've turned it on, you'll see the following option:

Step 1: Increase or decrease the volume by using the volume up or down key.

Step 2: Turn the feature on and off by tapping the symbol beneath the volume bar.

On a Samsung Galaxy smartphone, turn on Live Caption.

For this instruction, we utilized a Samsung Galaxy Note 20 running Android 11.

Step 1: Navigate to the Settings app, then pick Accessibility > Hearing Enhancements > Live Caption.

Step 2: You are now in the Live Caption menu. Turn the Live Captioning option to enable Live Captioning and begin receiving auto-generated subtitles.

But, before you go, take a look at the other options available. You can fine-tune your Live Captioning experience from here. Hide Show Sound Labels displays noises like laughing, clapping, and music in the subtitles, while Profanity covers obscenities and swearwords.

But it's the last option that we prefer. Volume Control with Live Caption adds a toggle button to your volume controls, allowing you to turn it on and off fast and simply.

After you've turned it on, you'll see the following option:

Step 1: To increase or decrease the volume, use the up or down arrow keys. To access the full volume control, tap the three horizontal dots at the top of the floating bar.

Step 2: Turn Live Captions by tapping the symbol in the top-left corner. The setting will be confirmed by a menu message.

How do I enable live caption on my android 10 device?

If you have an original Google Pixel, you have been excluded from the Android 11 upgrade and the wider rollout of Live Caption. On Android 10, though, you may still use Live Caption. This is how it is done.

Step 1: Start playing the video, audio, or anything that you wish to caption.

Step 2: Increase or decrease the volume by using the volume up or down buttons.

Step 3: Below the volume controls, you'll see a caption icon. When you tap it, a Live Caption box will display on the screen. If you don't see the symbol, go to Settings > Sound > Live Caption and make sure Live Caption is turned on under the volume control.

Step 4: You may move the caption box around the screen by tapping and dragging it.

Step 5: To turn it off, press the volume up or down button again and then hit the caption symbol.

If you want to use Live Caption all of the time, go to Settings > Sound > Live Caption and turn it on at the top. As a result, whenever speech is recognized, you will receive live subtitles. If you're using Live Caption for the first time, you'll get a notice that says, "Live Caption recognizes speech in media and automatically creates captions." This function consumes more energy when the media is played. All audio and captions are handled on the device and are never saved or sent to Google. Currently, only English is available."

How To Use The "Do Not Disturb" Mode On Android

Throughout the day, our cellphones grab our attention several times. Some individuals even check their phones at all hours of the day and night. Why do we allow this never-ending barrage of incoming alerts, many of which are irrelevant or, worse, email spam, to disrupt us? If you can't stand that flashing LED or buzzing in your pocket, you need to learn how to use Android's Do Not Disturb mode.

Don't give in to your smartphone addiction. Set some ground rules for your phone and make sure it doesn't annoy you at meetings, the theater, or when you're sleeping. Let's take a look at how to activate Android's Do Not Disturb mode.

Note: Menu options may change from phone to phone depending on the manufacturer, but Do Not Disturb mode is baked into standard Android and should be available on any Android device running Android 6.0 or later.

Do Not Disturb In Android 11: How To Use It

Do Not Disturb features a number of layers that you can adjust to enable some applications and chats to flow through while others are muffled. You may also make bespoke schedules that start and stop at specific times.

To enable Do Not Disturb mode, expand the Notification Shade by swiping down from the top, and then press the Do Not Disturb symbol, which looks like a minus within a circle, as seen above. Do Not Disturb will be activated based on your preferences.

Long-press on the Do Not Disturb symbol in the Notification Shade to access the Do Not Disturb settings. People, Apps, Alarms & Other Interruptions, and Schedules are the four primary components on the following screen. We'll go over how each one works.

Note: You may also get to these options by going to Settings > Sound & Vibration > Do Not Disturb.

People

There are 3 parts to this section:

Conversations

Tap the circle next to one of three discussions that can be interrupted after tapping Conversations:

- All Conversations
- Priority Conversations
- None

Swipe down to expand the notification shade and then long-press on the chat to make it Priority. By pressing the cog symbol within Conversations, you may also alter the configuration.

Calls

This part is quite simple. After you've selected Calls, press the circle next to one of the four contacts you're authorized to interrupt:

- Anyone
- Contacts with a Star
- Contacts
- None

If you expect someone to call again within 15 minutes, you can enable Allow Repeat Callers.

If you're not sure how to "star" a contact, try these steps:

Step 1: To use the Phone app, just tap it.

Step 2: At the bottom, tap the Favorites tab.

Step 3: In the upper right corner, tap Add.

Step 4: Choose a contact from the drop-down menu.

You may also launch the Phone app, go to the Contacts tab, press to open a contact, and then tap the hollow star in the upper right corner. You may also touch the cog icon next to

Starred Contacts and then Add Starred Contacts on the next page.

Messages

After selecting Messages, press the circle next to one of the four message types that can be interrupted:

- Anyone
- Starred Contacts
- Contacts
- None

To add someone to Starred Contacts or Contacts, press the cog symbol adjacent to those two categories.

Apps

By default, Google's Digital Wellbeing app shows on the list. However, you may touch the + sign next to Add Apps and then pick the app(s) that are permitted to interrupt from the list.

Alarms & Other Interruptions

This section is simply a set of a switch for enabling and disabling the following:

- Touch Sounds
- Alarms
- Media Sounds
- Calendar Events
- Reminders
- Toggle each one on or off by tapping on a toggle.

Schedules

Android 11 already has two schedules that are turned off by default. You may add a new schedule by pressing the + sign next to Add More, or you can edit the two that are currently, thereby tapping their respective cog symbols, as explained below.

Sleeping

This mode, by default, covers all seven days of the week, beginning at 10 p.m. and ending at 7 a.m. the next day.

Step 1: Next to Sleeping, tap the cog symbol.

Step 2: Press Days, then tap the box next to each day to deactivate or enable it.

Step 3: To set the start hour and minute, tap Start Time.

Step 4: Tap End Time to set the hour and minute for the end time.

Step 5: To switch this setting on or off, tap the switch next to Alarm Can Override End Time.

Step 6: Tap the switch next to Use Schedule to enable or disable this schedule.

Event

This option is enabled by default for each calendar event with an answer of "Yes or Maybe." To alter the default setting, perform the following steps:

Step 1: Tap the cog icon next to Event.

Step 2: Select Any Calendar, Family, or your Google Account under During Events For.

Step 3: Select Yes, Yes or Maybe, or Yes, Maybe, or Not Replied from Where Reply Is menu.

Step 4: Tap the switch next to Use Schedule to enable or disable this schedule.

Note: On the Schedules screen, tap Add More to add a new Event, Time, or Driving service.

Advanced

When you tap Advanced on the Do Not Disturb screen, two more options appear:

Duration for Quick Settings

There are three options here:

- Keep using it until you turn it off.

- Always inquire.

- For 1 Hour — Use the Plus and Minus symbols to modify the time between 15 minutes and 12 hours. When you're finished, press OK.

Display Options for Hidden Notifications

There are three options in this area. Activate the following setting by tapping the circle next to it:

- There is no sound from the notifications.

- Notifications have no visuals or sounds.

- Custom — If Custom is chosen, press the gear symbol next to it to activate or disable these six parameters.

How To Use Android 10's "Do Not Disturb" Mode

In Android 10, the Do Not Disturb Settings menu is changed. Three parts may be found here: Behavior, Exceptions, and Schedule.

BEHAVIORS

There are two parts in the Behaviors section:

Sound & Vibration

Turn the following three settings on or off by tapping the Toggle next to them when you hit Sound & Vibration:

- Touch Sounds
- Alarms
- Media
- Notifications

Tap the circle next to one of two settings after tapping Notifications:

- Silently Show Notifications – notifications will be muted.
- Hide Alerts – Even while the Notification Shade is open, most notifications will not be heard or viewed.
- To fine-tune the feature even further, tap the cog symbol next to Custom. Other settings like as Don't

Turn on Screen, Don't Blink Light, Hide Notification Dots, and others can be disabled.

Exceptions

Two components in the Exceptions section enable you to whitelist certain contacts or calls.

Calls

Tap the circle next to one of four call types that may interrupt after pressing Calls:

- From Contacts Only
- From Anyone
- None
- From Starred Contacts Only

You may modify starred contacts in the Contacts or Phone apps or go to the Starred contacts area below to do so, much like Android 11.

If you receive a call from someone more than once within a 15-minute period, there is a toggle that allows repeat callers to get through.

Messages, Events & Reminders

This section is similar to the Android 11 section. You may select who can interrupt you, if at all, by tapping the Messages option in this section:

- Starred Contacts
- Anyone
- Contacts
- None

While the Do Not Disturb mode is on, touch the switch next to Reminders and Events to deactivate or enable these alerts.

Schedule

There are two subsections in this section:

Duration

Select one of three choices from the Duration tab:

Until You Turn Off

for 1 hour The length of this option may be adjusted between 15 minutes and 12 hours using the Plus and Minus symbols.

Always enquire

Automatically turn on

This area enables you to switch on Do Not Disturb mode automatically during sleeping hours and meetings. In this area, you may also create custom rules depending on events or the time of day. When your Pixel phone recognizes that you are driving, you may activate Do Not Disturb mode. As required, you may turn it off here.

Step 1: To make a rule, tap Add rule.

Step 2: Decide if you want it to be an event or a time.

Step 3: Give it a name and then follow the on-screen directions to finish configuring it.

For Samsung phones

On Samsung phones running Android 10, the Do Not Disturb option isn't nearly as strong. You can turn it on and access the settings, in the same manner you do with stock Android, but your choices are limited. There are four major components in addition to the main Turn On Now toggle.

Turn On as Scheduled

To turn this component on or off, touch this option and then the toggle next to Sleeping. When you tap Sleeping (the default schedule), you'll see four options to tweak:

- Days
- Name
- End Time
- Start Time
- Tap Save to keep your changes.

Duration

This is comparable to how Android works out of the box. Tap Duration, then select one of three choices by tapping the circle next to it:

- Until I Switch It Off
- 1 Hour — Use the Plus and Minus symbols to modify the time between 15 minutes and 12 hours.
- Always inquire.
- Select OK to save your changes.

Notifications are turned off.

When you tap Hide Notifications, you'll see six toggles appear. Toggle these settings on or off by tapping each Toggle.

Allow Exceptions

You'll see a list of various options and toggles if you tap Allow Exceptions.

Step 1: Select one of the four choices under Calls From All, Contacts Only, Favorite Contacts Only, or None.

Step 2: Select one of the four choices for Messages From All, Contacts Only, Favorite Contacts Only, or None.

Step 3: Option the Repeat Callers toggle to allow or disallow someone from contacting you more than once every 15 minutes.

Step 4: Enable or deactivate Alarms, Media Sound, Touch Sounds, Calendar Events, and Reminders by tapping the toggle next to them.

Do Not Disturb on Android 9.0 Pie and Previous Versions

Swipe down from the top of your screen to access the Notification Shade and touch the Do Not Disturb icon, just as in the newer versions. You'll see a menu with three choices on most phones running Android 6.0 Marshmallow through Android 9.0 Pie:

Total silence: Nothing will be able to disturb you.

Only alarms: Any alarms you've set may cause you to be disturbed.

Only alarms will go through, but you may choose precisely what else should and shouldn't bother you.

You'll notice an option to select how long Do Not Disturb mode should be active underneath that. You may configure it to remain on for an hour to cover a meeting, select a time when it should turn off, or instruct it to stay on until you manually turn it off.

Setting Priority Notifications

You must first specify what a priority notice is if you wish to utilize the Priority only option.

Step 1: Open the Settings app by tapping.

Step 2: Select Sound & Notification from the drop-down menu.

Step 3: Select Do Not Disturb from the menu.

Step 4: Select Priority Only Allows from the drop-down

menu.

Its Settings > Sounds and Vibration > Do Not Disturb > Allow Exceptions > Custom if you have a Samsung Galaxy phone.

Step 5: Enable or deactivate Reminders and Events by tapping the toggle next to them.

Step 6: Select Anyone, Contacts Only, Favorites Only, Approved Contacts Only, or None from the Messages From menu.

Step 7: Select Anyone, Contacts Only, Favorites Only, Approved Contacts Only, or None from the Calls From menu.

Step 8: Toggle on or off the Repeat Callers function by tapping the toggle next to it. This enables a second call to be made within 15 minutes.

Setting Automatic rules

Set certain rules to make Do Not Disturb mode switch on automatically depending on an event or time.

Step 1: Open the Settings app by tapping.

Step 2: Select Sound & Notification from the drop-down menu.

Step 3: Select Do Not Disturb from the menu.

Step 4: Select Automatic Rules from the drop-down menu.

Note: If you have a Samsung Galaxy phone, be sure you complete the steps below: Enable as Scheduled under Settings > Sounds and Vibration > Do Not Disturb.

Step 5: Select Add Rule from the drop-down menu.

Step 6: Type a name for the rule in Rule Name.

Step 7: Go to Days and touch on the days of the week where you want the rule to apply.

Step 8: Select Start Time to determine when the rule will begin.

Step 9: To decide when the rule will expire each day, choose End Time.

Step 10: Toggle the Alarm switch on. If you'd want to activate or disable this function while in Do Not Disturb mode, you may Override End Time.

When you apply the Do Not Disturb feature to your whole calendar, the event-based rules you've set up in your settings will kick in, and place your phone in Do Not Disturb mode depending on your preferences. Distracting alerts will no longer interrupt scheduled conversations or meetings. Please keep in mind that this will only function for meetings or phone conversations that you have confirmed in advance.

Samsung Galaxy phones are now unable to apply these

event-based calendar restrictions to Do Not Disturb.

How To Use Focus Mode On Android

Google is rolling out a new feature called Focus mode in Android 10 called Digital Wellbeing, which provides a fantastic set of tools for overcoming phone addiction. You'll be able to choose which applications distract you the most, and activating Focus mode essentially stops them for the length of the mode's usage. You won't get any alerts and won't be able to utilize those particular applications as a result.

Google revealed a new feature with Android Pie that may help you break your smartphone addiction. The feature, dubbed Digital Wellbeing, includes a dashboard that displays the time spent on various applications and checking alerts, among other things. With Android 10, Google added a new Focus Mode to the Digital Wellbeing function, which is a really helpful addition.

This new mode enables you to choose a few applications on your phone that you believe waste most of your time and block them for a period of time so you can concentrate on something more useful.

What is Focus Mode?

Do Not Disturb has been clarified to become Focus Mode. It disables alerts from certain applications and prevents them from being used while the mode is enabled. As a result, you won't be able to launch a distracting app by mistake while working.

However, you will not lose your notifications since prior notifications, as well as notifications received while the concentrated mode was active, will be restored whenever you turn it off.

How to Use Focus Mode

First and foremost, check to see whether your phone has a digital wellness app. If it still doesn't have it, you can get it from the Play Store. To utilize focus mode on Android, follow these steps:

- Open the app from the app drawer or go to Settings and then Digital Wellbeing & Parental Controls.
- Now, go to the 'Ways to disconnect' section and touch on Focus mode.

- Select the applications that are the most distracting by checking the boxes next to them.

- You may now create a schedule by specifying a start time, an end time, and the days of the week after you've chosen your preferred time. Tap Set.

- Now, touch on Turn on Now to activate concentrate mode.

- By pressing a button on the notification shade, you may switch off the concentrated mode at any moment.

Take a break

For a limited period, you won't be able to access some applications. However, there is a 'take a break' option that allows you to utilize the app for up to 30 minutes while in concentration mode.

It may now take a long time to switch on Focus Mode by accessing the Digital Wellbeing app every time. You may add it to Quick Settings by dragging it down on your screen to access the Quick Settings panel and tapping on the pencil symbol in the bottom left corner. Scroll down the page until you locate Focus Mode, then hold and drag it into the menu to include it. You may now switch on Focus mode from your Quick Settings by just tapping on it.

ANDROID DARK MODE? AND HOW TO ENABLE IT

How to Enable Android Dark Mode on Android 10

The theming tint is set by default to the same wallpaper detection-based automatic mode as earlier Android versions, but there are no specific settings for a permanent color theme.

To use the dark theme on an Android 10 smartphone, follow these steps:

- Tap Display.
- Open the Settings app.
- Tap the toggle switch beside Dark Theme to enable it.

To access your fast settings, slide down from the top of your screen. The new dark gray backdrop with white lettering will be visible. Google Chrome, Google Play, and YouTube, for example, will automatically adjust to the dark look.

On Android 9.0 Pie, how do you enable Android Dark Mode?

The ability to choose between dark and light themes was introduced in Android 9.0 (Pie), although the procedure is a bit different than in Android 10.

To activate dark mode on Android 9, follow these steps:

- Open the Settings app and choose Display from the drop-down menu.
- To get a full list of choices, tap Advanced.
- Scroll to the bottom of the page and hit Device theme, then Dark in the pop-up dialog box.

Android 9 Dark Mode Limitations

The settings menu and other UI components, such as the alerts that appear underneath the quick settings, are colored in a light theme with a white backdrop and black lettering on Android 9. Dark mode may be used with a lighter background for a more consistent experience if you know how to alter your Android wallpaper.

Individual applications may be configured to their own dark

modes to complement the dark UI. A dark theme is available in a few Google applications, and it's pretty consistent with the quick settings dark UI.

How to Use Google Messages in Dark Mode

The Google Messages app utilizes the Android system's default theme by default, but you may select a different theme manually. Here's how to do it:

- Open the Google Messages application.
- In the upper-right corner of the app, tap the three-dot symbol.
- Select a theme.
- Tap OK after selecting the theme you wish to use (Light, Dark, or System default).

How to Enable Dark Mode for YouTube

YouTube has the same gloomy appearance. To enable it, follow these steps:

- In the top-right area of the app, tap your profile symbol.
- Go to the Settings tab.
- Select General.
- Toggle the Dark theme toggle switch. On a dark gray backdrop, you should now see video thumbnails, comments, and other text sections.

CHAPTER 6: HOW TO RECORD THE SCREEN ON AN ANDROID DEVICE

Want to record your screen or take a short video with your Android device? There are a variety of options for capturing a tape for friends or producing a video for professional reasons.

Taking screenshots is simple, but how about making a lengthier, more complex video clip of what's going on on your phone? If that's what you're looking for, here's how you record the screen on an Android smartphone, whether it's via an app, the built-in screen recorder on Android 11, or the in-built features on certain Android 10 devices.

On an Android 11 smartphone, you may record your screen.

Android 11 has finally included a native feature to record your phone's screen, which was hinted at in earlier versions of Android. Google's engineers opted to retain the feature when it was included in the Android 11 beta, so you may now record your screen on any Android 11 phone.

You must add the recording feature to your phone's Quick Settings menu in order to utilize it. To do so, access Quick Settings by swiping down twice on the Notification Shade. Then, in the bottom-left corner of the panel, press the Edit tile (it usually looks like a pencil). Before dragging the Screen Recorder tile into the Quick Settings area, find it. Finally, save the modification by tapping the Back arrow or swiping from the screen's edge.

You may now utilize the Screen Recorder by returning to the Quick Settings window. When you first start using it, you'll be asked whether you want to record sounds and display touches on the screen. After you've made your selections, press Start to start recording. When your phone starts recording, a red recording symbol will show in the notification shade. To stop the recording, pull down the shade and touch the Red symbol.

On an Android 10 smartphone, you may record your screen. The function of screen recording was a major addition to the Android 10 beta. However, it was removed before the final release. Thankfully, LG, OnePlus, and Samsung's user interface (UI) designers restored it.

On Samsung and LG smartphones, recording from the Quick Settings bar is possible.

The Quick Settings bars on Samsung and LG phones running Android 10 include a screen recording option. To reach the Quick Settings area, swipe down twice on your notification shade, then choose Screen Recording (on an LG phone) or Screen Recorder (on a Samsung phone). Then, to begin recording, press the Start button and wait for the brief countdown to end. Before the recorder can start recording, you may need to grant it certain rights, and LG cautions that any restricted material, such as Netflix, would be shown as a black screen with sounds. When you're done, use the Stop button to stop the recording.

Samsung takes things a step further with its recording choices, allowing you to include a face cam in your video. Simply touch the Front Camera symbol (which resembles a person's silhouette), and a tiny window displaying your front camera's stream will appear. If you're using a Galaxy Note phone, you'll be able to draw on the recording using the S Pen. To begin, just touch the Pencil symbol. You'll have to turn it off to interact with the screen properly again.

You can't seem to locate the option to record your screen in Quick Settings? Check to see whether your phone is running Android 10 and if it has been upgraded to the most recent version. Your updates will be available in the Settings app.

Using the Android 10 screen recorder on OnePlus devices

You'll be able to utilize a native screen recorder if you have a OnePlus smartphone running Android 10. It will not, however, be available via the Quick Settings bar at first. Instead, you'll have to add it as a shortcut first. Here's how you go about it:

Step 1: To access the notification drawer, swipe down on the status bar. To display all of the app tiles, swipe down one more time.

Step 2: To reach the next page, tap the Edit icon (it looks like a pencil), then swipe left.

Step 3: Drag the Screen Recorder app to the Quick Settings

menu by tapping and holding it.

Step 4: In the top-left corner, tap the Back button to save your changes.

When you enter Quick Settings after this, you'll be able to use the Screen Recorder.

Screen recording with apps

If you don't have an Android 10 smartphone from LG, OnePlus, or Samsung, you're out of luck. Don't worry. You won't have to purchase a new phone just to record your screen - just download an app that will perform the heavy lifting for you. A few excellent screen recording applications are listed below.

AZ Screen Recorder

The AZ recorder is a stand-alone recording app with no timers or watermarks. Best of all, it's easy to use and doesn't need any setup.

Begin by installing and launching the app. It will show a sequence of circles on your screen after it has been started, with choices for recording, screenshots, live streaming, and more. When you choose Record, you'll be prompted to confirm the screen recording. Swipe down on your device and touch the Stop button in your notifications to stop the recording after it's begun.

When you're not recording, the app's logo will remain superimposed on your screen so you can easily access it if necessary. Drag it down to the X at the bottom of the screen to delete it if you don't want it there. The floating button will appear after relaunching the app.

By clicking the floating button and selecting the gear-shaped symbol, you may access the app's settings. This will lead you to a menu where you may change various elements of video quality before you start recording, which is helpful if you require a certain quality or want to conserve space in your video files.

The software also has some small editing features and the ability to doodle on the screen while recording, making it an excellent choice for pros. You may also clip and edit the video, crop the screen as required, replace the soundtrack with anything you want, and convert portions to GIFs as needed. Before you're ready to share, go to this section to make any final adjustments.

Google Play Games

As the name indicates, this game management software is all about utilizing and documenting the games you play on Android. That means your first step should be to sign up for Google Play Games and explore the platform to find and play the games you want. Make sure you do this before attempting to record since Play Games only allows you to record games that are supported.

When you're ready, open the app and tap the game you'd like to record to bring up the Game details window. Then, to begin recording, touch the video camera-shaped symbol. After that, choose Next, and then select your video quality. Select Launch to begin gaming once everything appears to be in order.

The game will begin in a few seconds. Once you've arrived,

you'll have a variety of choices. By default, Play Games uses your front-facing selfie camera as a face cam, but you may disable it by pressing the video camera-shaped button. You may also silence the microphone by pressing the button. The most important thing to remember is that tapping the red Record icon will start your recording. To stop recording, touch the red Stop square on your facecam (or the Play Games logo if you're not using a facecam).

When you finish watching, your video will be immediately stored on your device. There's an instant share option labeled Edit & Upload to YouTube if you want to upload your video to YouTube. This step may take some time due to the limited editing capabilities of this app and the fact that it will record everything that appears on the device screen.

Screen Recorder & Video Recorder – XRecorder

If you don't like the others listed above, here's another third-party screen and video recorder. It was created by InShot and had over 100 million downloads and over 2 million reviews (boasting a score of 4.5 stars out of 5). It's easy to use; all you have to do is choose Video from the bottom menu and then touch the Record button to start recording your screen.

You may stop the recording by bringing up the Notification Shade at any time during the recording or by reentering the app and pressing the Stop button. You can also share your recordings and capture screenshots using the app, which includes a number of options you may tweak to your preference. There are quality options, audio deactivation, and the ability to change the orientation of your recordings among them.

XRecorder is free to download and use, although the free edition does include the odd pop-up ad. You may get rid of advertising for $6.

Mobizen Screen Recorder

Mobizen provides HD recording in a similar manner to the AZ app, so it's a nice alternative to try if AZ doesn't work for you.

The app may be downloaded and used from the app menu. The app will guide you through the process of creating an account, after which you will notice a small "air circle" icon on your screen. Mobizen will show you how to use it. When you're ready, press the record button to begin recording. (It's worth noting that the camera icon is just for taking screenshots.) Before the app begins recording, there will be a three-second countdown.

The air circle will be visible while you're filming, but it won't appear in the finished video. Select it once more and press the pause icon to pause the video whenever necessary. When filming, the topmost button has a red stop button that you may choose at any moment to stop the movie.

When you've finished recording, a pop-up window will appear, allowing you to preview your video. If you want to make changes, you can choose to edit from there. If you save your video, you may go back and make changes later. As you watch, a pen-and-paper editing symbol will appear underneath the film, and selecting it will allow you to modify your movie. You can trim and divide the video, add background music, add intros and outros, and make it appear just the way you want it to.

ADV Screen Recorder

ADV Screen Recorder is a free third-party program that enables you to record any screen activity. To control your recordings from any screen, tap the + symbol in the app to reveal the button overlay. Keep in mind that you won't be able to interact with the rest of the screen while this overlay is active.

When you activate the button overlay, you'll find options for starting recording, adding a front-facing camera view, accessing your video library, and drawing on the screen. Before you can use any of these capabilities, you must first give the app the necessary rights.

Start your video by tapping the record button, then stop or pause it using the button overlay. From inside the app, you may modify and share your recording. You may adjust the resolution (up to 1080p), bit rate (up to 15Mbps), and frame rate in the options (up to 60fps). You may also adjust the video and microphone settings.

The overlay may be customized by adjusting its opacity,

replacing the default icon with a custom picture and adding text, or entirely removing it. You may also allow the app to record screen touches, but you'll need to activate the functionality in your phone's settings first.

Even after you exit the app, the app's button overlay may stay visible on the screen. The only method to get rid of the overlay is to hold down the long-press button on it and drag it to the X at the bottom of the screen.

CHAPTER 7: PICTURE-IN-PICTURE ON YOUR ANDROID

Picture-in-Picture (PiP) is an Android feature that is accessible on devices running Android 8.0 Oreo or later. You can multitask with it. For example, you may use Google Maps to find a restaurant while video chatting with a buddy or view a humorous video on a website while using Google Maps to obtain directions. PiP is a useful tool for multitaskers who often switch between apps.

On Android, enable PiP Apps.

After that, make sure your Android apps are up to date:

- Go to the Settings menu.
- Select Apps & Notifications from the drop-down menu.
- Select Advanced > Special app access from the drop-down menu.
- Choose Picture-in-Picture from the drop-down menu.
- Select an app from the drop-down menu.
- Enable PiP by tapping the Allow picture-in-picture option.

Compatible Apps

Because picture-in-picture is an Android feature, many of Google's popular applications, such as Chrome, YouTube, and Google Maps, support it. YouTube's PiP mode, on the other hand, needs a paid membership to YouTube Premium, the company's ad-free premium subscription program. YouTube TV, the company's streaming TV service, also supports PiP mode.

Other compatible apps include:

- Hulu
- VLC
- Facebook
- Netflix
- WhatsApp
- Google Duo
- Instagram
- Pocket Casts

How to Launch Picture-in-Picture

Depending on the app, you may launch picture-in-picture in one of two ways:

Go to a webpage to start playing a video in full screen in Google Chrome, then press Home on your Android.

Some applications, such as VLC, need you to first activate the functionality in the app settings.

When you're on a video call on WhatsApp, touch the video preview to enable PiP.

PiP Controls

When you've worked out how to use PiP in your favorite program, you'll see a window in the lower-right corner of your screen containing your movie or other material.

To access the controls, tap the window. You'll see Play, Fast Forward, Rewind, and Maximize in certain instances. Full-screen mode returns you to the app in full-screen mode. To go to the next song in a playlist, touch the Fast-Forward symbol. Only Exit and Full-screen icons are available in certain videos.

To leave the window, drag it to the bottom of the screen and move it anyplace on the screen.

Some applications include a headphone icon that may be tapped to play music in the background without displaying visual content.

How to Share Wi-Fi Passwords From Android to Any Smartphone

Starting with Android 10, users of Google's mobile operating system may exchange Wi-Fi passwords by scanning a QR code. To scan the code and join the Wi-Fi network, the receiver just has to launch the default camera app on their iPhone or Android smartphone.

Navigate to your handset's Settings menu when you're ready to give access to your Wi-Fi network. Swiping down from the top of the device's screen to reveal the Quick Settings menu is the simplest method to accomplish this. The Settings menu will appear when you touch on the Gear symbol.

Because each Android smartphone is unique, you may need to slide down a second time to find the Gear symbol.

You may also reach the App Drawer by swiping up from the bottom edge of your phone. You can find and launch the "Settings" app here.

Then choose "Connections," "Network & Internet," or something similar. The name of this menu may vary based on the manufacturer of your Android device.

Now, from the top of the menu, choose the "Wi-Fi" option.

Make sure you're connected to the Wi-Fi network you wish to share with others, then pick the network name (SSID) or the Gear symbol that corresponds.

You've arrived at the network's Advanced Settings menu. Tap the "Share" or "QR Code" button. The button should be represented by a QR code symbol, regardless of what your smartphone names it.

Note: Before displaying a code, certain OEMs may ask you to enter your screen lock password/PIN/pattern/biometrics.

A QR code will now be generated and shown on your Android device. Allow your visitors to scan the code using the default camera app on their Android or iPhone. A message inquiring whether they wish to join the Wi-Fi network may appear.

CHAPTER 8: HOW TO USE ANDROID DEVICE MANAGER FOR REMOTE SECURITY ON ANDROID

Google's Android Device Manager app was recently upgraded to enable remote password changes as well as the ability to locate and erase your lost or stolen device. We'll show you how to do it here.

Apple customers have had the option to monitor their devices if they are lost or stolen for a long time.

The Find My iPhone feature has been lauded as a theft deterrent, with reports of individuals reclaiming their iPhones by showing up at the perp's home with the cops in tow.

Now, for GPS-enabled smartphones and tablets, Android has introduced a tool called Android Device Manager. It enables you to track down your misplaced smartphone, change passwords, lock screen PINs, and even erase it remotely.

Here's how to set up your phone or tablet to utilize the service so you can find your Android the next time it slips under the couch.

Setting up Android Device Manager

1. Go to www.google.com/android/devicemanager first, where you'll be asked to approve Google's request for location data. Because this is a tracking service, it is essential to complete this step in order for the functionality to function correctly.

2. If you already have a Nexus device that supports location services, it should appear on your list right away. The current location of your cellphone, as well as the last time it was used, is shown here.

3. To switch between devices, click on the name, which will bring up a drop-down menu. You'll be brought to the map screen for that model if you choose a different one. By clicking on the pencil symbol, you may rename each device.

4. To set up a new device, go to the Software Store on the device itself and search for the Android Device Manager app. Look for the one with the green circle and target in the center among a few similar applications.

5. When you tap the install button, you'll be sent to a new Welcome page that asks for permission to access your location data. If you wish to utilize the service, you must

consent to this, just as you did in Step 1. Accept the offer, and you're good to go.

6. Because the Android Device Manager software runs the service via the web interface, the screen now appears very similar to the one in Step 2. The drop-down option should display after your smartphone has detected a GPS signal.

7. You may now examine the features that are offered in more detail. There are two icons under the device name: Ring and Set up Lock & Erase. We'll take a look at each of them one by one, beginning with Ring.

8. Even if your smartphone is locked and set to vibrate, selecting the Ring option will enable the program to let it proclaim itself at maximum volume for five minutes. This is especially helpful if you've misplaced it elsewhere in the home.

9. Choosing Your Setup You'll see a dialog box informing you that you need to send the device a notice if you use Lock and Erase. Touch Send, and a message for Android Device Manager will display in your notification area; tap it.

10. You'll be directed to the app's settings, where you'll be asked whether you want to enable the device

administrator? If you agree, your device will get access to all of the security features.

11. The Lock option now allows you to set a new lock screen password remotely, while Wipe is the last resort option. It's essentially a factory reset that wipes your device clean of any data. In the case of theft, this device is very effective.

How to Remotely Wipe Your Stolen Android Phone

If you lose or steal your phone and are concerned that a criminal may get access to your data, you may have no option but to erase the data remotely.

You may have a high possibility of rendering your data worthless to the thief if your Android is linked to your Google account and the internet. Learn how to remotely wipe your Android phone and what to do to secure your device in advance to prevent someone else from accessing your messages, media files, and applications if your phone is lost.

Use Find My Device

If the idea of losing your phone makes you nervous, make sure you've planned ahead of time and have a way to track down your Android phone or wipe it if it's gone for good. Installing the Google Find My Device app is one option.

Find My Device is free software that allows you to safeguard your smartphone's data remotely. Apart from that, it may assist you in locating your phone if you lose it and allow you to contact the person who discovers it.

How to use Find My Device

Once you've downloaded and synced the app with your Android device, be sure to launch it and go through all of the permissions to enable Find My Device to monitor your phone's position.

If your phone is lost or stolen after that, you will have the following choices for recovering it and safeguarding your data.

Locate your phone

You may track down your missing phone by using the Google Find My Device app on another Android phone or by utilizing the program's web version.

When you log in, Find My Device will display the current position of your smartphone on a map, as well as the last place it reported when it had a signal. If your smartphone is turned off and does not have a signal, Find My Device will notify you of its position as soon as it is turned on and has a signal.

Find My Device includes a useful Play Sound option if the phone is within your grasp, but you still can't find it. Even if your phone is set to quiet, it will ring for 5 minutes, enabling you to find it more quickly.

Secure your phone

If you're certain you didn't simply lose your phone and are concerned about a stranger gaining access to it, you may utilize Find My Device to protect your sensitive data. On your lock screen, you may lock your phone, sign out of your Google account, and show a message containing your contact information. This may be very beneficial to the individual who discovers your gadget.

Erase your phone

Finally, you may remotely wipe your Android phone using Google Find My Device. It will erase all of the data on your device.

Because this is essentially a factory reset, you won't be able to utilize Find My Device to find your smartphone once you do this. You won't be able to recover your personal information, so create a backup of anything essential ahead of time.

Use Android Lost

Android Lost is a Google-unaffiliated third-party software that allows you to wipe your phone remotely. To register your device, just download and install the app on your phone.

In the event that your phone is lost or stolen, you may manage and monitor it using another Android phone or the Android Lost website.

How to control your phone with Android Lost

Take your smartphone and follow these steps to set up Android Lost: From Google Play, download and install the Lost Android app, then provide it access to your phone's location, contacts, and media files. Request Administrator privileges in the app to be able to manage your phone remotely. That's all you'll need to get Android Lost up and running on your phone.

What else can you do if your phone is stolen or lost?

Both Google Find My Device and Android Lost are excellent applications for controlling your smartphone from afar. However, Find My Device is better in that it can be used even if you don't have the app installed on your phone - either via the online version or by using the software on someone else's Android phone.

If you can't find your phone that way, you may use your Google Maps location history to attempt to find it. At the absolute least, you'll be able to figure out where you misplaced your phone or where it was before the battery died or was turned off.

The Android Device Manager is another popular method of erasing data from a phone. It's a built-in feature on every Android phone that allows you to delete all of your personal data.

You must first sync your Android device (smartphone or tablet) with the Android Device Manager in order to utilize this function. It works with Android versions 2.2 and above. To sync your device, follow these steps:

Go to 'Settings' on your phone and choose 'Android Device Manager.'

Select 'Allow Remote Lock and Factory Reset' from the drop-down menu.

Make sure the button labeled "Remotely Locate This Device" is selected. If you don't see it, click on it.

Check the option labeled "Allow Remote Lock And Factory Reset." After you've done that, a screen will appear asking for your permission to erase your device's data.

Enter your Google account to access Android Device Manager online, then choose the device you wish to sync.

After your device has been synchronized, follow these steps to erase the data from the phone:

1. Visit https://www.google.com/android/find on your computer and log in with your Google account credentials.

2. The Device Manager will try to find your phone after you've signed in. You should see a map with your device's position on it.

3. You may either 'Ring,' 'Lock,' or 'Erase' your device.

4. You will be prompted to create a new password if you choose Erase. Then a window will appear, alerting you of the danger. If you accept, your phone's complete data will be wiped.

Note: Only utilize this option if your device has been permanently lost.

Are there any constraints?

Yes, utilizing Android Device Manager has its drawbacks. For example:

1. Only if your device is linked to the internet will it function.

2. Android Device Manager will be useless if you have logged out of your Google account. This is the first thing they'll do if your phone is taken since everyone knows Android Device Manager can be used to find, lock, or delete data from the device.

3. It won't be able to load your device if you haven't enabled Android Device Manager on your phone.

CHAPTER 9: SPEED UP YOUR ANDROID PHONE BY TUNING THE ANIMATION SCALE

You're probably using a phone that's been around for at least a year. And, if industry patterns are to be believed, you'll most likely keep it for another year before upgrading. Your phone's current performance is either (still) a pleasant ride or an obstacle course, depending on where it was on the specifications scale originally.

You're definitely encountering delays and slowdowns in your everyday use if you didn't want to spend a lot of money in the first place and purchased a budget gadget a year or two ago. So, I'm going to teach you a simple technique that will help your phone run quicker and more responsive. At the very least, it will seem to be such.

Tuning the animation scale is one of the oldest techniques in the book when it comes to improving the performance of your smartphone. Continue reading to learn more about the animation scale, how to use it, and the advantages it provides.

What is the animation scale in Android?

The Window animation scale, Transition animation scale, and Animator duration scale are the three kinds of animation scales in your system. The animations that occur as you browse across a website, launch a window, or switch between screens are controlled by all three of these scales. You can figure out which choice is for what by looking at the names.

Resources are used by animations. As a result, the higher the value, the more work your CPU has to do. Obviously, you'll need to increase the animation size if you want clean, quick, and responsive animations. The visual experience will be improved, but there will be a price to pay. You'll have to make a sacrifice in terms of performance.

Because we're trying to speed up your phone, you'll probably want to reduce the size of the animations or turn them off entirely. Sure, scrolling and switching screens will be tedious, but it will seem that you are moving quicker.

In Android, how do you deactivate (alter) the animation scale?

Developer Options must be enabled in order to access the animation settings. If you already have Developer options enabled in Android, skip this step;

if not, follow these instructions to activate Developer options in Android:

- Go to the Settings menu.
- Scroll down to About phone and touch it.
- Locate the area under "Build Number."
- Continue pressing the Build number area until a pop-up message appears stating that you are now a Developer.
- After that, the Developer Options section will appear in the Settings.

Now that everything is in place let's get started. You're all set to experiment with animations. Here's how you can do it:

- To get started, go to Developer Options.

- Scroll down to find the Window Animation Scale, Transition Animation Scale, and Animator Duration Scale.

- You may experiment with all three choices to discover which one gives you the greatest results. From Off to 10x, any animation scale may be used.

- That's all; if you cut down the animations to 0.5x or turn them off entirely, your phone should feel quicker, but the transition between screens or scrolling will be flat.

CHAPTER 10: HOW TO MONITOR (AND REDUCE) YOUR DATA USAGE ON ANDROID

Increasingly smartphones and data-hungry apps make it simpler than ever to exceed your cellular plan's data cap. and pay expensive overage fees. Continue reading to learn how to control your data use better.

It would have been unthinkable of only a few years ago to go through several GB of mobile data. It's simple to burn through your data limit in a couple of days now that applications have expanded in size (it's not unusual for apps and their updates to surpass 100MB in size), and with streaming music and video becoming more popular.

A gigabit of data can quickly be used by watching one hour of standard definition streaming video on Netflix or

Youtube. When you upgrade that stream to HD, the bandwidth consumption almost triples–roughly three gigabytes of data will be consumed—using Google Play Music or Spotify to listen to high-quality music? For that, you'll need approximately 120MB each hour. It may not seem to be much at first, but if you do it for an hour every day for a week, you'll have accumulated 840MB. For a month, one hour a day adds up to around 3.2GB. If you have a 5GB data plan, you've already used around 65 percent of it on music.

You could pay extra for a more comprehensive package, but who wants to do that? Here are some tips for minimizing your data consumption before you spend your hard-earned money (and keeping an eye on it).

How to Check Your Data Usage

Before you do anything else, you should examine your data use. You have no clue how gently or seriously you need to change your data consumption habits if you don't know what your usual use looks like.

You may use Sprint, AT&T, or Verizon's calculators to obtain an approximate idea of your data use, but the best thing to do is examine your usage over the last several months.

Logging onto your cellular provider's online portal (or checking your paper bills) and looking at your data use is the simplest method to verify previous data usage. If you find yourself often over your data limit, contact your provider to see if you can switch to a less costly data plan. If you're approaching or over your data limit, you should certainly keep reading.

You may also use Android to check your current month's

consumption. Select Settings > Wireless & Networks > Data Usage from the drop-down menu. You'll see a screen that looks similar to the last one here:

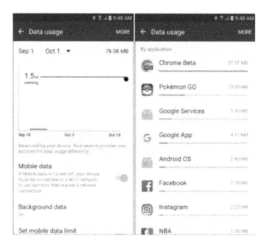

As shown in the second image above, scrolling down will reveal the cellular data consumption by the app. It's essential to remember that these graphs only display data transmitted over your cellular data connection, not over Wi-Fi. Even if you're a YouTube addict, if you view all of your videos while connected to your home network, it won't show up here. If you want to view your Wi-Fi data use as well, choose "Show Wi-Fi usage" from the menu.

It's worth noting that in order to get the most accurate view of your data consumption, you'll need to select your payment cycle here. Because your data will be reset on the first day of the new cycle, it doesn't matter what you used the previous month. Therefore you don't want it to bias your findings.

You may also configure data warnings by setting the slider bar to your preference—when you approach the amount indicated by the cutoff limit, you'll get a warning to let you know where you're at.

You may also select the "Set mobile data limit" option and then use the orange slider to determine where data should be entirely shut off. Once you've reached that limit, your phone's mobile data will be blocked until you switch it back on.

How to Keep Your Data Use in Check

When it comes to mobile devices, there are two types of data sinks. The first is user-driven data consumption, often known as "foreground data." If you're using mobile data rather than Wi-Fi, every time you view a high-definition movie or download a new album, you're directly adding to your monthly data consumption.

To consume fewer foreground data, you must actively reduce the amount of time you spend downloading, streaming, and surfing.

The relatively huge quantity of behind-the-scenes data flowing through your connection—the "background data"—is less apparent to most people. If you're not cautious, polling for Facebook updates, frequent email inbox checks, automated program upgrades, and other background activities may eat up a lot of your data. Let's see what we can do to mitigate some of this.

First: See Which Apps Are Using Data

Let's start by looking at which apps are really producing significant quantities of background data. To view your applications in order of data use, go to Settings > Wireless & Networks > Data Usage. Individual apps may be tapped for a more comprehensive look. We can see how the foreground and background are used in this example:

This will be very beneficial in the stages that follow. You can concentrate on correcting which applications use the most data if you know which apps use the most data.

Limit Background Data, App by App

If you don't want to utilize another software to accomplish these things, you can do a lot of the manual adjusting yourself to save data.

Return to your home screen and launch one of the applications that are using excessive data. Check to see if it has any data use restrictions. Instead of using Android to limit Facebook's data use, you may go inside the Facebook app and reduce the frequency of push notifications or disable them entirely. Not only does turning off alerts and continuous polling save you data, but it also extends the life of your battery.

However, not every program will offer these options–or as much fine-tooth control as you want. So there's another possibility.

Return to Settings > Wireless & Networks > Data Usage and choose an app from the list. Check the box titled

"Restrict Background Data" (with Nougat, there is just a switch named "Background Data," which you should turn off rather than on). This will restrict the amount of data it uses at the operating system level. This only applies if you're using a mobile data connection; if you're using Wi-Fi, Android will enable the app to consume background data as usual.

Turn Off All Background Data

If that isn't enough, you can also turn off all background data with a single switch—this will decrease your data consumption in most cases, but it won't distinguish between data sippers and data hogs, which may be inconvenient. You may check "Restrict Background Data" from the Data Usage menu by pressing the menu button. All background data for all apps will be disabled as a result of this.

Turn Off Background App Updates

Because Google understands how valuable your mobile bandwidth is, app updates–which may potentially use more data than anything else–will only happen automatically when you're connected to Wi-Fi, at least by default. Open the menu on the Play Store to check sure this is the case (and that you didn't alter it anywhere along the way). Make sure "Auto-update apps" is set to "Auto-update via Wi-Fi only" under Settings.

Before we continue, a brief note: when we speak about limiting background data use, we want to be clear that these limitations only apply to your mobile data usage; even if you severely restrict an application, it will continue to work properly while you are connected to Wi-Fi.

Purchase Your Favorite Apps (to Remove Ads)

Apps often have two versions: a free version with advertising and a premium version with no adverts. Developers must eat in order for you to compensate them with ad income or real cash. But here's the thing: advertisements aren't just irritating; they also waste data. These upgrades range in price from $0.99 to a few dollars, and they're well worth the money if you use the app often.

Use Chrome's Data Saver

If you often browse the web on your phone, Google Chrome's "Data Saver" option may help you avoid exceeding your data limit. Basically, it sends all of your data via a Google-run proxy, which compresses it before delivering it to your phone. Essentially, this not only reduces data consumption but also speeds up website loading. It's a win-win situation.

You were probably prompted to activate Data Saver the first time you launched Chrome, but if you declined, you might do so later by launching Chrome, going to Settings > Data Saver, and moving the toggle to "On."

Cache Google Maps Data

The easiest method to prevent using large amounts of data when out and about (and relying on cellular data) is to cache it while you're enjoying the benefits of a free Wi-Fi connection.

You're using a lot of data if you use Google Maps for everyday navigation or vacation planning. You may pre-cache your route rather than using the live-updating version (and save a ton of mobile data usage in the process). When you're ready to conduct some heavy Maps usage, open Maps while connected to the internet, open the menu, and choose "Offline regions." From there, you can either select "Home" to download maps around your home or "Custom Area" to download maps for any other locations you'll be visiting soon.

Use Streaming Apps with Offline Modes

Offline modes—modes that enable users to pre-cache data when on Wi-Fi to use while on cellular data connections—are being added to many streaming service applications. Offline options are available on Rdio, Rhapsody, Slacker Radio, and Spotify to assist users in avoiding exceeding their data limits.

Data Caching Is Your Friend

You may cache data in a variety of different places as well. Before you go out and about, think about how you can offload your data to Wi-Fi.

For example, we know it's every 2003, but there's something to be said for downloading music, podcasts, ebooks, and other material to your device from the convenience of your own home (and Wi-Fi connection).

How do I prevent any android app from using my mobile data?

Try limiting background data on Android if your applications consume a lot of mobile data. Here's how to save money by turning off data.

Do you try to minimize data consumption on your Android smartphone by avoiding needless downloads and live streams? But you can't figure out why so much of your mobile data disappear so quickly?

Here's the thing: even when you're not actively using an app, it may eat up data. But don't worry; Android has a feature that allows you to prevent any app from consuming data in the background. Third-party applications may make things even simpler and give you more choices.

The following are the different ways for limiting data consumption on Android:

1. Android's Built-In Option to Restrict Background Data

These methods will prevent applications on your Samsung, Google, OnePlus, or any other Android phone from utilizing data:

- Go to the Settings section of your phone. Swipe down from the top of your phone's screen to do this. Then, in the top-right corner, touch the settings symbol.

- Select Network & Internet > Data Usage from the drop-down menu. At the top of the menu, you'll see how much data you've used.

- To check how much data each app has used lately, go to App data consumption.

- Look through the list and choose the program that consumes the most data. You may be shocked at how much data YouTube alone consumes.

- To switch off cellular data for particular applications, toggle off Background data.

- If it isn't already turned off, turn off Unrestricted data. When the data saver is turned on, this keeps the app in check.

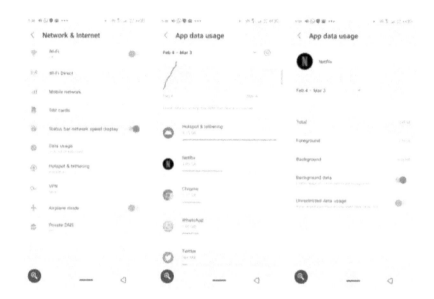

These methods allow you to limit applications to Wi-Fi exclusively and prevent bandwidth-intensive apps like YouTube from accessing mobile data.

Return to the Data use menu if you're more eager to keep your data consumption under control. Choose Data Saver. Then choose Use Data Saver from the drop-down menu. This setting limits your total mobile data use.

2. Set a Data Warning and Usage Limit

While the methods listed above are important for limiting your mobile data use, you should also consider establishing a data warning and usage restriction.

To do so, follow these steps:

- Tap Network & Internet in your phone's settings menu.

- Go to Data Usage > Data Limitation & Warning.

- Toggle on the Set data limit option.

- Navigate to Data Capacity. Choose GB or MB from the dropdown menu. Then, for your data use limit, enter a number.

- Also, turn on the Set data warning option.

- Warning about data. After that, type in a data warning value.

When you establish a data limit, your mobile data is immediately turned off when your use exceeds the amount you selected. The data alert simply informs you that your data use has exceeded the limit you specified before.

The data warning figure, on the other hand, should be within the range of your data limit. However, you may wish to make this number a bit closer to the data limit set.

The Third-Party Option to Restrict Data Usage on Android

Despite the fact that there are other third-party solutions that may help you manage your data use, we suggest NetGuard.

NetGuard is a firewall software that may block applications from connecting via Wi-Fi as well as utilizing cellular data. Essentially, it allows you to choose which apps should connect to the internet and which should not.

These features decrease bandwidth, conserve battery life, and may help you avoid app alerts, pop-ups, and advertisements, in addition to saving your mobile data.

How to Limit App Data Usage With NetGuard

All of your applications are listed alphabetically in NetGuard. Wi-Fi and mobile data toggles are located next to each app. As a result, you may choose to block access by pressing one or both connection types.

To restrict an app's usage of mobile data, touch the cellular data symbol on the far right.

If you don't want the app to connect to a Wi-Fi network, touch the Wi-Fi symbol right next to it. To prevent an app from utilizing data at all, choose both icons.

Tap the menu arrow to the left of each app for more detailed controls and exceptions.

You may then opt to enable the app to utilize cellular data while the screen is on, prevent data when roaming, or allow it in lockdown mode after choosing your preferred connection type.

The app does not show pre-installed applications for the sake of simplicity. However, in order for NetGuard to show system applications, you must:

At the top-right corner of the screen, tap the three vertical menu dots.

Select Advanced settings from the Settings menu.

Toggle the Manage system applications switch on.

If necessary, you may restrict data use on particular mobile network connections. You may also enable unlimited 3G use while restricting LTE and 5G usage. If you're dealing with a metered connection, there are also Wi-Fi options.

To get to these settings, go to Settings > Network options

and turn on or off the relevant options in that menu as needed.

NetGuard's capabilities go beyond just preventing mobile data. You can also use it to keep track of when applications try to connect to the internet. This may provide you with information on what your phone's apps are doing.

Enabling these options may prevent you from unpleasant shocks if you install items like games that need an internet connection without realizing it. Keep in mind, though, that you may also download games that do not need an online connection.

CHAPTER 11: HOW TO USE WI-FI DIRECT FOR QUICK FILE TRANSFERS ON ANDROID

Modern cellphones are jam-packed with functionality and can do almost every task imaginable. However, an unintended consequence of this is that many of these functions stay buried beneath the sub-menus and are never fully used. This is exemplified by Wi-Fi Direct. In this part, we'll explain what Wi-Fi Direct is and how you may have been using it without realizing it.

What is Wi-Fi Direct?

The easiest way to describe Wi-Fi Direct is that it is a kind of direct device-to-device connection. Unlike 'traditional' Wi-Fi, which requires users to connect multiple devices to a centralized device (such as a router), Wi-Fi Direct allows users to connect one device to another directly (hence the term Direct). Because it utilizes the same security protocols as our regular Wi-Fi connections (WPS and WPA/WPA2), it's called Wi-Fi Direct.

Wi-Fi Direct is a kind of second-generation Wi-Fi that enables compatible devices that don't have their own internet connection to form a shared connection with those that do (Hotspots, modems, or routers). You may create a wireless network between many devices using Wi-Fi Direct. Additionally, you may screencast onto another device with a display via Wi-Fi Direct and Miracast. NFC is also supported by the latest version of Wi-Fi Direct.

A broad range of devices, including smartphones, tablets, computers, digital cameras, and televisions, enable Wi-Fi Direct. The Samsung Galaxy S (released in 2010) was one of the first smartphones to offer this function, and beginning with Android 4.0 Ice Cream Sandwich, all Android devices have it built-in. In case you were wondering, Apple devices also support Wi-Fi Direct, although under the names AirDrop and AirPlay.

Wi-Fi direct, to put it another way, enables devices that don't have their own internet connection to connect to one that does. You can connect Android smartphones and gadgets and transfer data fast and easily without the need for wires. Is Wi-Fi Direct just a more advanced version of Bluetooth? In a nutshell, yes and no. The benefit of Wi-Fi Direct over Bluetooth is that the Wi-Fi range and transfer rates are much faster. To summarize, if you want a faster method to transfer files from one device to another, utilize Wi-Fi Direct.

What is Wi-Fi Direct used for?

As of 2021, the functionality is utilized for a variety of applications, including file sharing and data transmission, screen sharing, and even multiplayer gaming. Let's have a look at some instances of use scenarios.

1. File sharing between phones

It wasn't easy to share big files across cellphones only a few years ago. Bluetooth and cable were your only choices. While sharing tiny files over Bluetooth worked OK, sharing bigger ones required waiting many minutes (or hours) for the transfer to finish. Data transfers through cables were quicker, but they were inconvenient. Large file transfers between cellphones (and even laptops/computers) have gotten considerably simpler with the introduction of Wi-Fi Direct.

Wi-Fi sharing may also be used to transfer data from an old phone to a new phone while the latter is being set up for the first time.

2. Wireless Printing

Wi-Fi Direct is supported by most contemporary printers, allowing them to connect wirelessly with computers and smartphones and effortlessly handle wireless printing tasks.

3. Playing games and screen-sharing

Offline, close-range smartphone gaming and screen-sharing are some of the other areas where Wi-Fi Direct has been widely utilized. Yes, you read it correctly. Wi-Fi Direct is responsible for your phone's wireless screen sharing capability. Some games utilize the same functionality to allow players to play multiplayer games without needing to be connected to the internet.

How to set up Wi-Fi Direct

Wi-Fi Direct is available on any Android smartphone running Android 4.0 or above (bar some very rare exceptions). While the user interfaces of the systems may differ, setting up this capability is very straightforward and consistent across all devices. Until recently, Wi-Fi Direct didn't have native file transfer capabilities. Thanks to a recently released functionality called Nearby Share, this is no longer the case. Google also offers its own 'Files' app, which features a file-sharing feature (which uses Wi-Fi Direct).

Wifi direct is a new technology that allows us to transmit data wirelessly in a similar manner as Bluetooth, but at a considerably quicker pace. Wifi direct provides the same "find, couple, and transmit" capabilities as Bluetooth. Wi-Fi direct, on the other hand, is not as widely used as Bluetooth at present. Some gadgets may not support Wi-Fi directly. In this demonstration, we'll utilize a Samsung Galaxy phone and a Huawei smartphone, both of which support Wi-Fi directly. There aren't any third-party applications needed.

Also, both devices must be in the same physical area, but there is no need for an Internet connection.

Step 1: Wi-Fi Direct allows you to connect two phones at the same time.

There seems to be some variation in how it is done among devices. In general, navigate to Settings > Wi-Fi, switch on Wi-Fi on your Android phone using the toggle, and then turn on Wi-Fi Direct. You may think of WiFi Direct as a Wi-Fi version of Bluetooth or a Wi-Fi file transfer. Before you can use Wi-Fi Direct, you must first activate Wi-Fi on your phone.

On a Huawei phone, the Wi-Fi Direct option is located at the bottom of the screen, next to a list of all available Wi-Fi networks. Touch Wi-Fi Direct to search for nearby Wi-Fi devices.

To activate Wi-Fi Direct on my Samsung Galaxy phone, go to Settings > Wi-Fi > More > More menu (three vertical dots) > Wi-Fi Direct > Wi-Fi Direct Your phone will then look for additional Wi-Fi direct devices to connect to.

To send a connection invitation to a mobile phone, tap its name in the Available Devices list. Accept the invitation on the second Android phone and connect the two Android phones using Wi-Fi Direct.

In the Available Devices column, the status of a phone connected through WiFi direct changes from Available to Connected. You may now transmit files between the two phones using Wi-Fi direct.

Step 2. Send and receive files via Wi-Fi Direct

On Android phones, Wi-Fi Direct is typically found under the Share or Action menu, among Bluetooth, Email, and other file-sending options. You may share chosen pictures and videos from the Gallery app by tapping Share > Wi-Fi Direct, then selecting a Wi-Fi Direct connected device. You may choose any file(s) from your phone's files manager to transmit over Wi-Fi Direct.

A Wi-Fi Direct Incoming Files notice may appear on the recipient device. Confirm that you want these files when you get this notification. On certain devices, the files may be received automatically without the need to confirm.

The files received through Wi-Fi Direct may be saved to a different path or folder on various Android phones. The normal Download folder on my Samsung phone gets all incoming Wi-Fi direct file transfers; on my Huawei phone, a new folder named Wi-Fi Direct was established to hold all Wi-Fi Direct files and documents.

Share files with Wi-Fi Direct on Android

You can transfer files between Android phones without using Wi-Fi Direct in a variety of ways. You can use Bluetooth to connect two Android phones and then share data between them. Email is a convenient method to send data to many devices. Many third-party applications, including as AirDroid, SHAREit, Transfer Anywhere, and ES File Explorer, enable us to send files wirelessly across many devices for no cost.

How To Send File Via Wifi Direct:

- Goto setting > Connection > Click Wifi >Tap Wifi direct
- Oen Gallery > choose Image > select share icon
- Tap WiFi direct > Tap mobile name > Tap connect
- Done

Now I will show how to do it on the old devices:

- Choose a setting icon.

- After that, go to All and choose WiFi.

- Now connect to the internet through wifi.

- Then, in the upright corner, tap the three dots.

- Wifi direct should be selected.

- Select the picture you wish to share from the gallery. Select the share icon.

- Go to WiFi Direct and choose it.

- To transmit the file, click on the device's name.

Note: Images and videos are simple to transfer, but what about apps? Don't worry; I'll teach you how to distribute applications through wifi direct as well. It's simple. Simply follow the steps below.

How To Send Apps Via Wifi Direct:

- Es file explorer may be downloaded through the Google Play Store.

- Open the es file and choose applications.

- You can now view all of your applications. Select any app by clicking and holding it.

- To generate a backup APK file, tap the Backup icon.

- Now go to the File Manager and choose Phone Storage from the drop-down menu.

- Tap on Apps after selecting the backups folder.

- There's a copy of your backup file there. Now pick it and press the share button.

- Now choose wifi direct on the second phone and make sure it's turned on.

- Choose the other phone number, and the file will begin to transfer.

How To Transfer Files Using Wifi Direct From Android To PC 2021

Es is a file explorer software that you may download and install.

Make sure your phone and computer are both connected to a wifi network, or turn on data on your phone and link your PC to your phone's hotspot.

Now launch the app and choose the three dashes in the top left corner.

Choose View on PC from the drop-down menu.

Now, press the switch on the button and copy the FTP address that appears; don't give it to anybody else.

Open Google Chrome or another browser on your PC and enter this FTP URL into the search box. All of your files will appear as soon as you paste the address.

To transfer files from your phone to your computer, first click on the file, then choose the place on your computer where you want to store it.

Screen Rotation Lock

Do you have Android 9.0 Pie? Why should you disable auto screen rotation?

Are you one of the fortunate few who have received the Android Pie update? The new Android operating system looks stunning and has a slew of simple enhancements, one of which eliminates the annoyance of auto-rotating the screen.

Smartphone users all over the globe know how inconvenient it is to have Auto-rotate switched on since even the tiniest shift in the phone's orientation may cause the whole screen to switch to landscape mode at inappropriate times. In the most recent version of Android, Google offers an easy solution for this, which includes turning off Auto-rotate entirely.

Setting up screen rotation

You can only turn Auto-rotate on or off in earlier Android versions. Place your phone in landscape position after it's turned on, and the app will adapt to that mode. If you turn it off, all apps will remain in portrait mode. It's easier to keep it off than to deal with random screen rotations, but putting it back on when you require landscape mode isn't quick.

The new approach in Android 9.0 Pie is simpler and easy to use. If you have the update, disable Auto-rotate first. Swipe down to see the notification drawer, then press on the Auto-rotate fast settings tile to turn it off. Your phone is now locked in one orientation only.

Using screen rotation lock

Open any app you want to use and rotate your phone to a landscape position after the screen rotation lock is deactivated in the notification drawer (certain applications, like Instagram, don't support landscape mode). The program won't switch to landscape mode, but you'll see a new icon appear to the right of the home button. It is shaped like a rectangle with two arrows pointing in opposing directions. When you tap it, the app will switch to landscape mode. If you now convert back to portrait orientation, the identical symbol will display. Return to portrait mode by tapping it one more. Because you don't have to swipe down to access the notification drawer, this is a significantly quicker way to switch between screen orientations. Only Android 9.0 Pie and later versions of Android have the new screen rotation functionality.

CHAPTER 12: HOW TO PAIR YOUR SMARTWATCH WITH AN ANDROID PHONE

New fantastic Smartwatches have been launched onto the market as a result of technological advancements, and this has piqued the curiosity of many. Sony, Samsung, and Huawei, among others, have all played a key role in the development of today's diverse range of smartwatches. The smartwatch has a touch screen interface and can do a number of activities that a traditional watch cannot.

Smartwatches, in reality, are capable of performing tasks that are quite similar to those of smartphones. It is said to include certain mobile applications and to be capable of connecting to Wi-Fi and Bluetooth. Smartwatches may also be used as portable media, as well as for making and receiving phone calls and texts, among other things.

You may couple the two devices using one of two ways. They're all simple to understand and follow. If you choose a technique that is practical for you, you will be able to establish a successful connection.

The following are some of the methods:

Method 1: Bluetooth Basic Pairing

This is the simplest technique of linking your Android phone to your wristwatch. As a consequence, all you have to do now is turn on Bluetooth and follow the following instructions:

Step 1: Make sure your Android phone's Bluetooth is turned on.

To guarantee a successful connection, make sure your phone's Bluetooth is turned on. To accomplish this, complete the following steps:

On your Android phone, open the Settings app.

Navigate to Bluetooth and choose it.

Toggle the Bluetooth toggle to the on position.

Step 2: Select "Discoverable Mode" from the drop-down menu.

You'll also need to enable the discoverable mode on your phone to make it visible to other devices. As a result, you will accomplish this by following the steps described below:

On your phone, open the Settings app.

Turn on Bluetooth by clicking on it.

Check the option to enable Discoverable mode under it.

Step 3: Put your Smartwatch on.

You must also make sure that your Smartwatch is turned on before beginning the pairing procedure. So, find the power button and push it repeatedly until it turns on. The pairing screen will then be displayed, featuring icons for a phone and a watch.

Step 4: Connect your Android phone to the smartwatch.

After that, you'll need to link your smartwatch with your phone. You must follow the steps below to couple the two devices:

PRO TIP: If the problem is with your computer or laptop/notebook, use Restore Repair to check the repositories and repair any corrupt or missing files. This works in the vast majority of instances when the problem is caused by a system flaw.

Navigate to the Bluetooth screen on your phone.

While Bluetooth is switched on, go to the bottom of the screen and choose Search for Devices or Scan Devices.

Select your Smartwatch from the list of devices.

Following that, a new screen with a code will appear. Make sure the code on your phone and the code on your wristwatch are the same. To link the two devices, go to your phone's settings and choose Pair.

Your wristwatch and Android phone are now successfully linked and ready to use.

Note: To ensure a successful connection, make sure your devices are in close proximity. Also, if you want to use all of your watch's features, you'll need to use third-party applications like Smart Connect.

Method 2: Use of SpeedUp Smartwatch

Additionally, this technique is another simple way to connect your SpeedUp wristwatch to your Android phone. All you have to do now is download the SpeedUp app and follow the instructions below:

Step 1: Install the SpeedUp Smartwatch app on your smartphone.

You must first download and install the SpeedUp Smartwatch app from the Google Play Store on your phone. The app is also available for download on the company's website. To get the app from Google Play, follow the instructions below:

Go to the Google Play Store and download the app.

Look for SpeedUp Smartwatch on the internet.

Install should be selected.

Step 2: Turn on your phone's Bluetooth.

Then, while you prepare for the connection, switch on Bluetooth on your phone. You must follow the procedures outlined in Method 1 to do this.

Step 3: Select "Discoverable Mode" from the drop-down menu.

Then, by turning on discoverable mode, you'll be able to make your phone visible to other devices. To do this, be sure to complete the procedures outlined in Method 1.

Step 4: Open the SpeedUp Smartwatch app on your smartphone.

To prepare for connection, launch the SpeedUp app on your phone and follow the onscreen instructions. Then, in the list of devices, look for its name and complete the pairing procedure.

Step 5: Connect your Android phone to your SpeedUp Smartwatch.

To quickly connect your devices on your phone, follow the instructions below:

Make sure Bluetooth is turned on.

To get the Bluetooth name of your smartwatch, open the SpeedUp smartwatch app on your phone and go to Search Smartwatch. When the name Bond displays, click it.

When the pairing notification displays on your phone, touch the tick symbol on your watch and then select Pair.

After a short time, the pairing will be successful. To double-check, press the Send notice button on your phone, and if it vibrates, it indicates the connection was successful.

Things You Didn't Know Your Smartwatch Could Do

A smartwatch is basically a tiny computer that can do incredible things on your wrist. In reality, modern smartwatches are capable of far more than simply checking the weather, seeing incoming messages, and playing a few Android Wear games. Users may be shocked to learn that Android Wear smartwatches can do certain high-end James Bond-style tasks.

1. Customize your watch face

The watch face is really very important, considering how frequently you'll be engaging with your smartwatch. You may either use the ones that were pre-installed on your smartphone or download third-party apps from Google Play. If you really want to get creative, there are a number of applications that enable you to create your own watch face.

Once you've installed your favorite watch faces, you'll be able to change them anytime you like. Simply press and hold your finger on the main screen until the device vibrates and the watch face choices display. Swipe through the choices until you find the one you want. You'll also see a + symbol, which is where you may add downloaded watch faces. You may delete a watch face by swiping up or down on the screen if you feel it's no longer working for you.

Remember that personalizing your watch face entails more than just picking a design or theme that you like. You'll be in control of personalizing the difficulties as well. This means you have complete control over what information appears on the watch face. If you want to see your steps, heart rate, and the weather, for example, you may arrange the complications appropriately.

2. Connect to Wi-Fi

This may seem self-evident, but you must connect your new Android wristwatch to the internet. This connection will be required for many of the things you'll want to utilize to work correctly. If your device supports Wi-Fi, you may access the settings by swiping down from the top of the screen. Select Wi-Fi from the connection menu. The next step is to create a network. If a password is needed, you must input it before choosing to connect on your phone.

Going the future, you may change the Wi-Fi option to automatic, which means your watch will automatically connect to the stored network when it becomes available. You can access essential functions without needing to have your phone close at all times after you've established this connection. You'll benefit from having your watch linked to Wi-Fi whether you're browsing the Google Play Store or setting reminders with Google Assistant.

3. Download and pin apps

Wear OS has gone out of its way to pre-install certain applications on your wristwatch. However, you'll almost certainly want to add to that list. There are a few approaches to this. If you find yourself depending on your wristwatch for even the most basic activities, you'll probably be satisfied with downloading applications from the Google Play Store.

You may be better off doing this from your phone or computer if you're having trouble navigating the tiny screen. However, if you can do it directly on your watch, it will take fewer steps. You may access the app menu by pressing the side button or the crown once you've completed installing the applications. You may also find that pinning the applications you use the most is beneficial. Hold your finger down on the icon of the app you wish to pin while you browse among applications. Your app will rise to the top of the list, with a star next to it. When you wish to unpin an app, follow the same steps.

4. Configure your keyboard

Your phone may not always be available, whether you're taking a short note or responding to a message. Maybe you're in a situation where utilizing Google Assistant to accomplish the task isn't the best option. Whatever the situation may be, there are a few different keyboard setup choices available to assist you.

Wear OS comes with three default options: a rudimentary keyboard, handwriting, and voice. Some users may find that the standard keyboard is sufficient for quick, brief responses on the move. It's a different thing when you're typing on a little screen for an extended period of time. The handwriting option enables you to write on the touchscreen with your finger. If you don't want to bother with the basic keyboard or handwriting, you may use your voice instead.

Swipe down from the main screen and touch the gear symbol after it's installed. You'll choose input methods after navigating to customization. You should see a keyboard management option. You may pick and choose which ones you wish to utilize. When using an app that requires a keyboard, you may now press and hold the keyboard icon. You'll see a selection of possible choices, from which you may choose the keyboard you wish to use. Fortunately, Google Play has a plethora of keyboards to choose from.

For the standard Google keyboard, you may also modify your settings. Do you want auto-correction and auto-capitalization to be enabled? It's no issue. If you want to go that far, there's also the option for next-word ideas. At the very least, this will make using the standard keyboard a little simpler.

5. Personalize buttons

Your Android wristwatch may feature a single side button, or it may have a primary button and a few others, depending on the model. These buttons may be customized to launch your favorite applications. From the main screen, swipe down and touch the gear icon. Scroll down to

Personalization and choose Customize Hardware Buttons from the drop-down menu. You may need fast access to Google Play or your favorite music app. You'll be able to start that app with just one click after you've customized it.

6. Manage notifications

Don't forget to handle those alerts now that you've finished customizing your new Android wristwatch to your taste. When you receive an email, text message, or app notification, you probably don't want your wrist to vibrate. Not to mention the fact that notification overload depletes the battery.

By using the Wear OS app on your phone, you may choose which alerts you want to receive on your watch. When you're in the settings area, go to notifications and choose to modify your watch notifications. You may choose which applications you wish to get alerts from here. Keep the alerts that are important to you and delete the others.

7. Preserve battery life

While Android smartwatches excel in a variety of areas, battery life isn't at the top of the list. One of the most common criticisms about Wear OS is its poor battery life across the board. Sure, your watch keeps track of a lot throughout the day, but do you really need to charge it every night? What a pain in the neck.

There are a few things you can do to help your Wear OS watch's battery last longer. By swiping down on the main screen for a percentage, you may check the state of your battery. You may launch the Wear OS app on your phone for additional details. Select watch battery from the settings menu to show how much battery is left till it's time to recharge. This will also show you which applications are using the most battery life.

Many Wear OS smartwatches include energy-saving modes that turn off non-essential functions to assist prolong battery life. There's also a time-only option that turns everything off but the clock. It renders your smartwatch almost worthless, but it's still alive, right? There are less extreme methods to extend the life of your battery. For example, you may switch off the always-on display, deactivate tilt-to-wake, dim your screen, turn off unnecessary alerts, and so on.

8. Choose your music apps

One of the greatest Wear OS features is the ability to listen to music from your watch using Bluetooth headphones. Spotify and Deezer are two popular alternatives. Simply go to the Google Play Store and download your favorite music applications. These applications may already be loaded on many Wear OS devices. If Bluetooth headphones aren't accessible, you can play music from your wrist if you have a Wear OS watch with a built-in speaker.

As you may be aware, now that YouTube Music has replaced Google Play Music, your watch's offline music storage is in jeopardy. When it comes to saving music for offline listening on your phone, this isn't a huge issue, but it isn't accessible on Wear OS yet. Until we learn more about future plans, we'll have to make do with these alternative music applications.

9. Take advantage of Google Assistant

Google Assistant is another noteworthy feature of Wear OS that you should make use of. You can operate your watch with your voice. Press and hold your watch's primary button while speaking your instruction. You may also activate Google Assistant with the conventional "OK Google" voice command if you want. This will need allowing Google Assistant to listen to your voice. Be aware that this function is known to deplete the battery rapidly.

If you're new to Google Assistant, just ask, "What can you do?" and you'll be given a complete list of instructions. Making phone calls, sending text messages, obtaining directions, setting timers and reminders, and monitoring workouts are just a few of the popular choices.

10. Set up Google Pay

You'll be able to make payments straight from your watch if your smartwatch supports Google Pay. This means you won't have to spend time digging through your wallet for that one credit card or rummaging through your pockets for cash. You must first add your cards to the appropriate app on your watch.

Select get started in the Google Pay app on your smartphone. You'll next add a card by following the on-screen directions. You'll need to add a card to your watch if your phone already has one. After you've completed this procedure, you'll be able to use that card to access Google Pay from your watch. Simply open the app on your watch and hold it over the payment terminal whenever you're in a location that supports Google Pay. If you're given a choice to pick between credit and debit, go with credit. It's as simple as that!

CONCLUSION

Apple may have started the smartphone revolution, but Google is the one who has brought it to its logical conclusion. Android has surpassed Windows and macOS to become the most popular computer platform on the planet, outnumbering iOS. This is due in large part to the fact that it is an open-source project with a lot of power. Android is extremely strong, although it may become a little perplexing at times. Google is always tweaking Android and adding new features, and OEMs like Samsung and OnePlus may add their own features on top of that.

Because of its powerful capabilities, Android is by far the most popular and versatile mobile operating system available. The greatest part is that it allows you to personalize the gadget to your liking. With the appropriate applications from the Google Play Store, and apparently, basic Android phones can become a melting pot of technology and creativity.

Do Not Go Yet; One Last Thing To Do

If you liked this book or found it useful, I'd appreciate it if you could leave a quick review on Amazon. Your support is greatly appreciated, and I personally read all of the reviews in order to obtain your feedback and improve the book.

Thanks for your help and support!

Ingram Content Group UK Ltd.
Milton Keynes UK
UKHW021300120423
420044UK00020B/628

9 798529 381762